The Directory of Chicago Area Ethnic Organizations and Media

Third Edition

Copyright ©2012 by Chicago Area Ethnic Resources
All rights reserved. This book or any portion thereof
may not be reproduced or used in any manner whatsoever
without the express written permission of the publisher.

Printed in the United States of America
ISBN 978-0-615-61671-1
Chicago Area Ethnic Resources
PO Box 2204, Glenview, IL 60026
www.chicagoethnic.org

To inquire about quantity discounts for libraries, schools, government agencies and other institutional needs, please contact the publisher at admin@chicagoethnic.org.

Chicago Area Ethnic Resources is a nonprofit, 501 (c) (3) organization, founded to help the mainstream public understand and respond to diversity and changing demographics and to give voice to the ethnic communities that call our region home.

TABLE OF CONTENTS

Organizations by Ethnic Group

	Page
African	7
African American	7-13
Arab American	14-15
Asian American	16-18
Assyrian American	18
Bangladeshi American	19
Belizean American	19
Bosnian American	19
Cambodian American	20
Cameroonian American	20
Chinese American	21-23
Congolese American	23
Croatian American	24
Czech American	25
Dominican American	25
Dutch American	26
Eritrean American	26
Ethiopian American	26
Filipino American	27
Finnish American	27
German American	27-29
Ghanaian American	29
Greek American	30-33
Guatemalan American	33
Haitian American	34
Hispanic/Latino	34-47
Indian American (Asian)	47-50
Iranian American	50
Iraqi American	51
Irish American	51
Italian American	52-56
Japanese American	56-57
Jewish American	58-67
Korean American	68-71
Lao American	71
Latvian American	72
Lebanese American	72
Liberian American	73
Lithuanian American	73-75
Muslim American	76-77
Native American	78-79
Nigerian American	79
Norwegian American	80
Pakistani American	80-81
Palestinian American	82
Polish American	82-87
Puerto Rican	87
Romanian American	88
Scandinavian American	88
Scottish American	89
Slovak American	89
Somali American	90
Sudanese American	90
Swedish American	90-91
Tibetan American	92
Ukrainian American	92-93
Vietnamese American	93
Multiethnic	94-98
Government Agencies	98-99

Ethnic Media

	Page
African American	100-104
Arab	104
Chinese	105-6
Danish	107
Filipino	107-8
German	108-9
Greek	109-10
Hispanic/Latino	110-15
Indian (Asian)	116
Irish	117
Italian	117
Japanese	118
Jewish	118-19
Korean	119-20
Lithuanian	121
Pakistani	122
Polish	123-24
Russian	125
Multiethnic	126

Also Available from Chicago Area Ethnic Resources

The Chicago Area Ethnic Handbook

A Guide to the Cultures and Traditions of the Metropolitan Area's Diverse Communities.
Second Edition

"A fascinating walk through the neighborhoods of Chicago ethnic groups."

Chicago Sun-Times

Updated and Expanded!

The Ethnic Handbook, second edition, is required reading for anyone seeking to get a handle on the diverse groups that call our region home. With in-depth profiles of the major ethnic communities in Chicago and the suburbs, this one-of-a-kind guide is filled with facts and information, including: updated demographics, historical narratives, issues for the communities, holidays and special events, migration patterns, special health concerns and more.

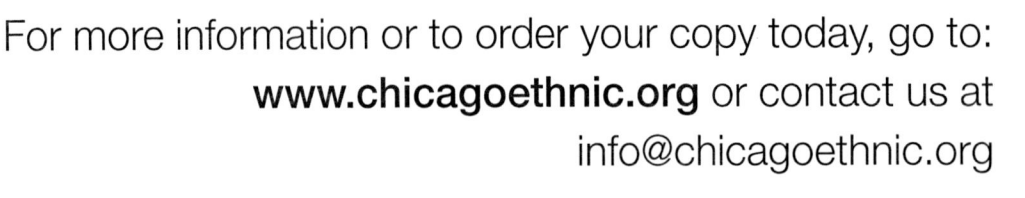

For more information or to order your copy today, go to:
www.chicagoethnic.org or contact us at
info@chicagoethnic.org

Introduction

Welcome to the third edition of the *Directory of Chicago Area Ethnic Organizations and Media*, the region's most comprehensive resource on the ethnic organizations that serve the Chicago area's diverse populations. The Directory has been completely updated and offers professionals of all stripes an invaluable tool for reaching out to the organizations and media that define this global city and its environs.

When we began this project back in the '90s, under the auspices of the Illinois Ethnic Coalition, our mission was to showcase the many ethnic organizations that defined the social, political, economic and cultural landscape of the nation's third largest city. We knew our work would not only tell a story on its own, but would serve the metropolitan area in a broader way by providing information on and access to diverse networks that spanned across the counties.

Now produced by Chicago Area Ethnic Resources – a spinoff of the Ethnic Coalition – the Directory is the result of many hundreds of research hours consolidated into one comprehensive, user-friendly document, presented both in print and electronic form. From social service organizations focusing on basic human needs to others providing immigrant acculturation, health outreach, civil rights advocacy, economic empowerment, education, culture preservation and more, you will find them here.

We are indebted to the interns and volunteers who helped us get this project off the ground and into print, specifically: Chris Bentley, Molly Born, Brandon Campbell, Shanika Gunaratna, Gina Harkins, Yoonj Kim, Noreen Nasir and Jean Williams. Matthew Holzman and Ann Weigand of 2plustoo Marketing and Design spent many hours consulting and assisting with layout and production. We also deeply appreciate the input of key non-profit leaders and public officials who provided feedback and guidance.

This project would not have been possible without the CAER board of directors, which provided encouragement, insight and financial support, and the Walter S. Mander Foundation, whose initial funding gave the project legs.

This Directory is the companion publication to *The Chicago Area Ethnic Handbook,* second edition, which profiles in 37 chapters the demographics, histories, socio-economic and cultural characteristics of the region's most prominent ethnic groups. Used in tandem, the Directory and the Handbook provide the wider public with a deeper understanding of the fabric of our community.

Jeryl Levin, President
Cynthia Linton, Editor

Chicago Area Ethnic Resources

AFRICAN

The Pan-African Association

6163 N. Broadway
Chicago, IL 60660
(773) 381-9723

Contact:
A. Patrick Augustin
exec. dir.
Email: apaugustin@sbcglobal.net

Purpose:
To serve, empower and promote the interests of refugees and immigrants of African descent.

Programs:
Workforce development, citizenship and civic education, computer vocational training, cultural, health outreach, mentoring, drivers ed.

Website: www.panafricanassociation.org

United African Organization

3424 S. State Street, Suite 3C8-2
Chicago, IL. 60616
(312) 949-9980, -81

Contact:
Alie Kabba
exec. dir.
Email: info@uniteafricans.org

Purpose:
To promote social justice, civic participation and empowerment of African immigrants and refugees in Illinois.

Programs:
Disability services, senior services, child support, food stamps, citizenship services, ESL, housing services, youth programs.

Website: http://uniteafricans.org

(See also Cameroonian, Congolese, Eritrean, Ethiopian, Ghanaian, Liberian, Nigerian, Somali, Sudanese)

AFRICAN AMERICAN

Alpha Kappa Alpha Sorority

5656 S. Stony Island Ave.
Chicago, IL 60637
(773) 684-1282

Contact:
Deborah L. Dangerfield
exec. dir.

Purpose:
To promote friendship among college women and to be of service to all mankind.

Programs:
Black family, health, global poverty, economic security, social justice, human rights, leadership training.

Website: www.aka1908.com

AFRICAN AMERICAN

Bethel New Life, Inc.

4950 W. Thomas
Chicago IL 60651
(773) 473-7870

Contact:
Sarah Spoonheim
sr. dir. of resource dev.
Email: info@bethelnewlife.org

Purpose:
To help create a healthy, sustainable community on the West Side.

Programs:
Economic development, housing for seniors, job readiness training, financial literacy classes, foreclosure prevention assistance, adult daycare, community safety, advocacy, housing, computer training and office skills, small business center, health care for mothers and children, in-home services for seniors, mentoring program for youth, WIC.

Website: www.bethelnewlife.org

Black Contractors United

12000 S. Marshfield
Chicago, IL 60827
(773) 483-4000

Contact:
Belinda Henderson
Email: bcunewera@att.net

Purpose:
To expand the base of minority contractors; to help them achieve parity in the free marketplace without the restriction of bias or prejudice; to increase the success potential of new or existing firms by providing quality professional, technical and managerial assistance; to help a selected number of firms reach higher levels of growth, development and profitability through focused assistance; to act as a liaison between minority and majority contracting communities to the benefit of both.

Programs:
Monthly informative meetings, affirmative action/consulting/monitoring, some technical, managerial and educational training to members, referral, membership assistance.

Website: www.blackcontractorsunited.com

AFRICAN AMERICAN

Black Ensemble Theater

4450 N. Clark St.
Chicago, IL 60640
Phone: (773) 769-4451

Contact:
Jackie Taylor
founder and exec. dir.
Email: blackensemble@aol.com

Purpose:
To foster racial harmony by producing theater that attracts a diverse audience, involving them in a process that inspires interracial respect.

Programs:
Stages plays that have a positive statement, deliver a message across racial barriers, and educate as well as entertain; Outreach Program with schools; Little City Program that uses theater to increase cognitive, learning and developmental skills of participants; Community Access Program.

Website: www.blackensembletheater.org

Black United Fund of Illinois

1809 E. 71st St., Suite 200
Chicago, IL 60649
(773) 324-0494

Contact:
Henry L. English
pres. and CEO
Email: english@bufi.org

Purpose:
To provide funding, technical assistance and support services to projects and programs that address the critical needs of African-American communities statewide. Most services are provided primarily to community-based organizations but targeted services to individuals are offered.

Programs:
Philanthropy, business and professional support, technical assistance, grants, project and fiscal management, community development, capacity building, job training.

Website: www.bufi.org

Bronzeville Children's Museum

9301 S. Stony Island Ave.
Chicago, IL 60617
(773) 721-9301

Contact:
Pia Montes
Email: bronzvlle@aol.com

Purpose:
It is the first and only African-American children's museum in the country for all children ages 3 to 9 years old. Our mission is to expose and educate children and adults about the history, culture and contributions of African-Americans through hands-on, interactive exhibits and unique programs.

Programs:
Black History Month, Juneteenth, Kwanzaa, guided tours.

Website: www.bronzevillechildrensmuseum.com

AFRICAN AMERICAN

Centers for New Horizons

4150 S. King Drive
Chicago, IL 60653
(773) 373-5700

Contact:
Dr. Sokoni Karanja
founder, pres. & CEO
Email: info@cnh.org

Purpose:
To help families build self-reliance and contribute to the revitalization of their community.

Programs:
Daycare, workforce development, counseling (family and individual), community and economic development, foster care and adoption services, senior citizen services, home daycare provider services.

Website: www.cnh.org

Chicago Urban League

4510 S. Michigan Ave.
Chicago, IL 60653
(773) 285-5800

Contact:
Andrea L. Zopp
pres. and CEO

Purpose:
To work for economic, educational and social progress for African Americans and to promote strong, sustainable communities through progressive advocacy, effective collaboration, and innovative programming.

Programs:
Education, entrepreneurship, housing, human capital development, workforce development and diversity, health and wellness, policy and research.
Other facilities: Englewood office: 845 W. 69th Street

Website: www.thechicagourbanleague.org

Cosmopolitan Chamber of Commerce

203 N. Wabash, Suite 518
Chicago, IL 60601
(312) 499-0611

Contact :
Carnice Carey
exec. dir.
Email: info@cosmococ.org

Purpose:
To provide economic development, training and development for entrepreneurs.

Programs:
Advocacy, networking, counseling, economic development, education, mentoring, referral, technical assistance.

Website: www.cosmococ.org

AFRICAN AMERICAN

DuSable Museum of African American History

740 E. 56th Place
Chicago, IL 60637
(773) 947-0600

Purpose:
To collect, preserve and display artifacts and objects that promote understanding and inspire appreciation of the achievements, contributions, and experiences of African Americans through exhibits, programs, and activities that illustrate African and African American history, culture and art.

Programs:
Arts, children, culture preservation, education, heritage/history, literacy, research.

Website: www. dusablemuseum org

Kenwood-Oakland Community Organization

1005 E. 43rd St.
Chicago, IL 60653
(773) 548-7500

Contact:
Jay Travis
exec. dir.

Purpose:
Through the sustained engagement of low-income and working families, KOCO develops multi-generational leaders who impact decision-making process and public policies, improving the quality of life in our local communities.

Programs:
Community organizing around: youth investment, quality education, affordable housing, and senior services; emergency food pantry; youth development programs; employment training and placement; anti-hunger network; and emergency referrals.

Website: www.kocoonline.org

AFRICAN AMERICAN

League Of Black Women

254 Cove Drive
Flossmoor, IL 60422
(708) 754-1676

Contact:
Sandra Finley
board chr. & ceo
Email:
sfinley@leagueofblackwomen.org

Purpose:
To help women advance their professional leadership growth. Focus is on enhancing women's leadership power in the workplace, family and community. To conduct innovative research and produce proprietary leadership education programs supporting women's advancement ambitions, locally, regionally and globally. To help corporations provide pathways to success for black women as sought-after thought leaders and professional leadership talent. To support public policy measures that help ready the larger society for the contributions of black women's leadership engagement.

Programs:
Annual New World Power Global Leadership Conference, monthly Leadership Education webinars, League On Tour corporate education events, Leadership Research and Education.

Website: http://events.leagueofblackwomen.org

NAACP – Chicago Southside Branch

10540 S. Western Ave., Suite 201
Chicago, IL 60643-2529
(773) 429-9830

Contact:
Constance Morrow
sec.
Email:
cmorrow.h@sbcglobal.net
chicagossnaacp@gmail.com

Purpose:
To fight racial discrimination in the areas of education, housing, employment and police brutality.

Programs:
Legal referrals, referrals to city and state service agencies, monitoring government agencies and programs affecting blacks and others, educating community about racial unrest and crime, following legislation affecting community.

Rainbow/PUSH Coalition

930 E. 50th St.
Chicago, IL 60615
(773) 373-3366

Contact:
Candace Brown
ofc. mgr.
Email: info@rainbowpush.org

Purpose:
To protect, defend, and gain civil rights by leveling the economic and educational playing fields, and to promote peace and justice around the world.

Programs:
Work on issues such as poverty and hunger, peace and justice, gun violence, home foreclosure, criminal justice, corporate inclusion, voter registration.

Website: www.rainbowpush.org

AFRICAN AMERICAN

United Negro College Fund, Inc. (UNCF)

105 W. Adams Street, Suite 2400
Chicago, IL 60603
(312) 845-22100

Contact:
Jann W. Honore
regional dev. dir.
Email: jann.honore@uncf.org

Purpose:
General and operating funding for member colleges.
Programs:
Raise funds, to keep costs low and educational quality high.
Website: www.UNCF.org

Westside Assn. for Community Action

3600 W. Ogden Avenue
Chicago, IL 60623
(773) 277-4400

Contact :
Gloria Jenkins-Harvey
exec. dir.

Purpose:
To strengthen family ties, enhance individual and group problem-solving skills, encourage leadership development and promote collaborative partnerships with other social service agencies, neighborhood groups, block clubs, business and local government to promote human and community growth and development of Westside communities.
Programs:
Multi-service community-based network of 35 groups and organizations and 135 individuals.
Website: www.wacanetwork.com

The Woodlawn Organization

6040 S. Harper
Chicago, IL 60637
(773) 256-2905

Contact:
Warren Beard
lead comm. organizer
Email: info@twochicago.org

Purpose:
To preserve the community's strength and to maintain power to deal effectively and efficiently with those problems that harm wholesome community living.
Programs:
Child care, adult skill training, social services, rehab facilities, community empowerment, Woodlawn Community Development Corp.
Website: www.twochicago.org

ARAB AMERICAN

Arab Amer. Action Network

3148 W. 63rd. St.
Chicago, IL 60629
(773) 436-6060

Contact:
Hatem Abudayyeh
exec. dir.
Email: info@aaan.org

Purpose:
To provide social services and educational programs to the Arab American community.

Programs:
English as a Second Language, youth programs such as after-school boys and girls club, translating, public benefits assistance and case management, citizenship assistance, domestic violence referrals, and family literacy.

Website: www.aaan.org

Arab American Business and Professional Association

7101 N. Cicero Ave., Suite 203
Lincolnwood, IL 60712
(312) 834-4076

Contact:
Talat Othman
pres.
Email: abpa1991@a-abpa.org

Purpose:
To provide networking, business and professional services.

Programs:
Special business-interest seminars, dinners, luncheon speakers, business delegations to Middle East, receiving business and government officials from Middle East, translation, newsletter, networking.

Website: www.a-abpa.org

American Arab Anti-Discrimination Committee Chicago Chapter

8855 S. Robert Road
Hickory Hills, IL 60457
(847) 489-7999

Contact:
Abder Ghouleh
pres.
Email: rayhanania@comcast.net

Purpose:
To help American Arabs and all Americans confront discrimination, bigotry and bias. We strive to protect the right to free speech without fear of retribution, and the right to engage in activities and programs that support American Arabs while protecting this nation's civil rights.

Programs:
Public policy and political rights advocacy for Arab Americans, speaking events, dinners.

Website: www.adcchicago.com

ARAB AMERICAN

Arab American Association of Engineers & Architects

P.O. Box 1536
Chicago, IL 60690-1536
(312) 409-8560

Contact:
Bilal Almasri
pres.
Email: aaaea@aaaea.org

Purpose:
To help its members succeed in their professions by networking through seminars and social activities. It is non-political and non-religious. It is open to all architects, engineers and computer science professionals of Arab heritage.

Programs:
Academic review courses, technical seminars, scholarship programs for students, networking.

Website: www.aaaea.org

Arab American Family Services

9044 S. Octavia Ave.
Bridgeview, Il 60455-2126
(708) 599-2237

Contact:
Itedal Shalabi
exec. dir.
Email:
info@arabamericanfamilyservices.org

Purpose:
To provide accessible and effective social services to communities and empower, educate and support individuals and organizations to foster economic well-being among Arab Americans.

Programs:
Advocacy, case management, community health education and research, cultural diversity training, domestic violence, elderly, immigration, internships, therapy and counseling, youth development.

Website: www.arabamericanfamilyservices.org

ASIAN AMERICAN

Apna Ghar, Inc.
4753 N. Broadway, Suite 632
Chicago, IL 60640
(773) 334-0173

Contact:
Serena Chen Low
exec. dir.
Email: info@apnaghar.org

Purpose:
To provide emergency shelter and support services for South Asian and immigrant women and children, victims of domestic violence.

Programs:
Emergency shelter; counseling; supervised child visitation; 24-hour crisis hotline; community education on violence and prevention; case management for transportation, health care, legal advocacy, technical assistance; translation; access to educational and vocational training and other life skill enhancement services.

Website: http://www.apnaghar.org

Asian American Bar Association of the Greater Chicago Area
321 S. Plymouth Court
Chicago, IL 60604
(312) 775-2044

Contact:
Mehpara A. Suleman
pres.
Email: aabachicago@yahoo.com

Purpose:
To represent the interests of the Asian American community and attorneys; to foster the exchange of ideas and information among association members and with other members of the legal profession.

Programs:
Legal.

Website: www.aabachicago.com

Asian Human Services, Inc.
4753 North Broadway, Suite 700
Chicago, IL 60640
(773) 293-8430

Contact:
Abha Pandyav
CEO
Email: kdeguzman@ahschicago.org

Purpose:
To meet critical mental health and social service needs of Asian-Americans.

Programs:
Primary Health Care Clinic, charter school (grades pre-K through 8), outpatient mental health counseling, job placement, legal services access, HIV/AIDS programs and health education, ESL classes, youth counseling and mentoring.

Website: http://ahschicago.org/

ASIAN AMERICAN

Asian American Institute

4753 N. Broadway St. Suite 502
Chicago, IL 60640
Phone: (773) 271-0899

Contact:
Tuyet Le
exec. dir.
Email: aai@aaichicago.org

Purpose:
To empower the Asian American community through advocacy by utilizing education, research and coalition building.

Programs:
Legal advocacy, community organizing, leadership development.

Website: www.aaichicago.org

Nat. Asian Pacific Center on Aging Chicago, Senior Environmental Employment Program

122 S. Michigan Ave., Suite 1414
Chicago, IL 60603
(312) 913-0979

Contact:
Mei Lin
Email: napcachicago@sbcglobal.net

Purpose:
To give workers age 55 and over the opportunity to use their skills in creative and meaningful jobs, to recognize talented older workers, to supplement EPA staff.

Programs:
Recruits, screens, hires and pays older workers, develops appropriate assignments in EPA offices, translating.

Website: napca.org

South Asian Progressive Action Collective

Contact:
Email: info@sapac.org

Purpose:
To take up progressive issues pertinent to South Asia and the Diaspora through direct action, creative expression, and discussion.

Programs:
Artistic expression, public education, media outreach, community dialogues, political and social discussion.

Website: www.sapac.org

ASIAN AMERICAN

South-East Asia Center

1134 W. Ainslie St., School Office
5120 N. Broadway, Social Services
Chicago, IL 60640
(773) 989 7433, School and Admin;
(773) 989-6927, Social Services

Contact:
Fanny Wong, *Social Services*
Run-Hao Hu, *Principal*
Raymond Lau, *Adult Daycare*
Email: seac1134@yahoo.com

Purpose:
To build bridges between Old and New World cultures and serve the needs of SE Asian and other immigrant and needy groups.

Programs:
Adult daycare, in-home services, full-day/ full-year child care, heating/cooling assistance, ESL, citizenship exam preparation, immigrant resettlement and adjustment, community center, community organizing, economic development, youth employment, health care, referral, research, senior citizens, cross-cultural bridge building, translating, technical assistance, tutoring, youth, business support, counseling.

Website: http://www.se-asiacenter.org/

(See also Bangladeshi, Cambodian, Chinese, Filipino, Indian, Japanese, Korean, Lao, Pakistani, Tibetan, Vietnamese)

ASSYRIAN AMERICAN

Assyrian National Council of Illinois

2450 W. Peterson Ave.,
Chicago, IL 60659
(773) 262-5589

Contact:
Isho Lilou
exec. dir.
Email: info@ancil.org

Purpose:
To serve and support not only the Assyrian community but other ethnic groups as well.

Programs:
Educational, welfare, cultural, health, youth job training, translating.

Website: www.ancil.org

BANGLADESHI AMERICAN

Bangladesh Association of Chicagoland

P.O. Box 59849
Chicago, IL 60659
(708) 612-6041

Contact:
Shafiq Rahman
pres.
Email: srahman60154@yahoo.com

Purpose:
To promote the culture.

Programs:
Children, cultural, community organizing, immigration, political, picnic for elderly, translating (Bengali to English and English to Bengali).

Website: www.bacillinois.org

BELIZEAN AMERICAN

Belizean Day in the Park Committee

9405 S. Throop
Chicago, IL 60620
(773) 881-0412

Contact:
Sylvia Manderson
Email:
belizedaycommittee@chicagobelizedayinthepark.org

Purpose:
To sponsor an annual Belize Day in the Park and scholarship fund for students of Belizean descent.

Programs:
Cultural preservation, arts, financial aid, heritage/history, community organizing, citizenship, social, health care.

Website: www.chicagobelizedayinthepark.org

BOSNIAN AMERICAN

Bosnian & Herzegovinian American Community Center

1016 Argyle St.
Chicago, IL 60640
(773) 989-4381

Contact:
Fadila Campara
exec. dir.
Email: info@bhaccchicago.org

Purpose:
To help Bosnian refugees and immigrants, and others from the former Yugoslavia adjust to their new lives in the United States by providing them with the services and resources that they need to successfully integrate.

Programs:
Outreach and interpretation (assistance with AABD, food stamps, Medicaid, TANF), social services for elderly (Circuit Breaker and housing), health promotion and education, cultural celebrations, citizenship preparation and assistance with application process, ESL classes, CEDA.

Website: http://www.bhaccchicago.org

CAMBODIAN AMERICAN

Cambodian Association of Illinois

2831 W. Lawrence Ave
Chicago, IL 60640
(773) 878-7090, ext. 201

Contact:
Dary Mien
exec. dir.

Email:
dary@cambodian-association.org

Purpose:
To serve the needs of a highly traumatized, limited-English speaking refugee group.

Programs:
Arts, counseling, children, citizenship, community center, community organizing, culture preservation, education, employment, family, immigrant resettlement and adjustment, literacy, referral, senior citizen, tutoring, women, youth, translating.

Website: www.cambodian-association.org

CAMEROONIAN AMERICAN

Cameroonian Brothers Association

P.O. Box 408849
Chicago, IL 60640
(847) 271-2357

Contact:
Louis Guiamatsia
Email: info@cabac.org

Purpose:
To help students by providing advice and help with registration, choice of classes, getting a part- or full-time job and finding a good neighborhood for an apartment; to promote cultural education.

Programs:
Advice to students, $300 to graduates, soccer training and tournaments, barbeques and picnics, celebration of Camroon's Independence Day, social events.

Website: www.cabac.org

CHINESE AMERICAN

Chinese-American Museum of Chicago
Raymond B. & Jean T. Lee Center
    238 W. 23rd Street
    Chicago, IL 60616
    (312) 949-1000
Contact:
    Anita Luk
    exec. dir
    Email: office@ccamuseum.org

Purpose:
    To promote the culture and history — through exhibitions, education, and research — of Chinese-Americans in the Midwest.
Programs:
    Exhibitions, education, research.

Website: www.ccamuseum.org

Chinese American Bar Association of Greater Chicago
    950 Milwaukee Ave., Suite 335
    Glenview, Illinois 60025
    (312) 606-3916
Contact:
    Beibei Que
    pres.
    Email: beibei.que@gmail.com, info@cabachicago.org

Purpose:
    To foster the exchange of ideas and information among members and others in the legal profession, the judiciary and the community; encourage and promote the professional growth of members; provide fellowship; provide and promote coordinated legal services to the Chinese and Asian community in the Chicago metro area; and encourage inter-cooperation with other organizations of minority/ethnic attorneys.
Programs:
    Legal.

Website: www.cabachicago.org

Chinese American Service League
    2141 South Tan Court
    Chicago, IL 60616
    (312) 791-0418
Contact:
    Bernarda Wong
    pres.
    Email: adminis@caslservice.org

Purpose:
    To be a nurturing hub within the heart of Chinatown and connect families and individuals of all ages with the vital support they need to flourish physically, economically, mentally and socially, enabling them to thrive and contribute to the greater Chicago community.
Programs:
    Social services, counseling, daycare, after-school programs, employment and training, housing and financial education, health programs, elderly services, immigration and naturalization.

Website: http://www.caslservice.org

CHINESE AMERICAN

Chicago Chinese Cultural Institute

P.O. Box 5505
Chicago, IL 60680
(312) 842-1988

Contact:
Z.J. Tong
Email: info@chicagocci.com

Purpose:
Chinese language and culture education, cultural exchange between Chicago and China.

Programs:
Chinese arts and cultural events, language classes, cross-cultural training, Chinatown tour, translation.

Website: www.chicagocci.com

Chinese Consolidated Benevolent Association of Chicago

250 W. 22nd Place
Chicago, IL 60616
(312) 225-6198

Contact:
Peter Chan
Email: ccbachicago@comcast.net

Purpose:
To be a liaison to and work for the welfare of Chinese living in America.

Programs:
Golden Diners Club, volunteer home delivery of meals, free clinic, food sanitation program, Chinese cemetery, Chinese school, Confucius Center, special events.

Website: www.ccbachicago.org

Chinese Fine Arts Society

Sherwood Conservatory Building
1312 South Michigan Ave.
Chicago, Ill 60605
(312) 369-3197
Email: info@ChineseFineArts.org

Purpose:
To promote the appreciation of Chinese culture, enhance cultural exchange and pursue excellence in Chinese music, dance and visual arts.

Programs:
Annual Chinese Music Concert series, Chinese New Year celebrations at Navy Pier and Daley Plaza, Music Festival in Honor of Confucius competition and concert, international music composition competition, Barbara Tiao composition competition (for students), QiXi, Rhythms of China concert, other community engagement programs.

Website: www.chinesefinearts.org

CHINESE AMERICAN

Chinese Mutual Aid Assoc.

1016 W. Argyle St.
Chicago, IL 60640
(773) 784-2900

Contact:
Steve Brunton
exec. dir.
Email: Steveb@chinesemutualaid.org

Purpose:
To enhance the socioeconomic well-being of the ethnic Chinese in Chicago and encourage their participation and contribution to American society.

Programs:
Adjustment counseling, literacy, citizenship, educational, Chinese culture and language classes, refugee immunization, youth, employment, literacy, social services, translating (for a fee).

Website: http://www.chinesemutualaid.org/

CONGOLESE AMERICAN

Congolese Community of Chicago

2069 W. Roosevelt Street
Wheaton, IL 60187
(773) 818-4904, (773) 320-7780

Contact:
Claude Bambi or
David Bamlango
pres.
E-mail: info@congochicago.org

Purpose:
To help integrate people of Congolese descent into American society while providing a platform for learning about and appreciating the richness of Congolese culture in its diversity.

Programs:
Speakers bureau, business support.

Website: www.congochicago.org

CROATIAN AMERICAN

Croatian Cultural Center
2845 W. Devon Ave.
Chicago, IL 60659
(773) 338-3839
Contact:
Nada Vasilj
Email: hkcenter@sbcglobal.net

Purpose:
To be a charitable, social and cultural organization.
Programs:
Charitable, social, cultural.

Croatian Ethnic Institute
4851 S. Drexel Blvd.
Chicago, IL 60615
(773) 373-4670, (773) 203-1368
Contact:
Ljubo Krasic
pres.
Email: croetljubo@aol.com

Purpose:
To maintain a central collection on Croatians and their descendants; to collect and preserve publications and artifacts relating to the ethnic heritage of 2.5 million people of Croatian descent in the U.S. and Canada; to promote and develop curricular materials for the study of ethnic heritage; to conduct research on the Croatian and other European migrations.
Programs:
Culture preservation, education, heritage/history, language, referral, research.
Website: www.croatian-institute.org

Croatian Women, Branch No. 1 Chicago
2241 N. Janssen
Chicago, IL 60614
(773) 525-8571
Contact:
Nevenka Jurkovic
pres. & exec. dir.
Email: croatian_woman@yahoo.com

Purpose:
All-purpose organization.
Programs:
Art exhibits, citizenship, community organizing, culture, preservation, foreign aid, heritage/history, immigrant resettlement and adjustment, language, recreation, social, financial aid, translating.
Website: http://hrvatskazena.org, www.croatian_woman.org

CZECH AMERICAN

Czechoslovak Heritage Museum, Library and Archives
122 W. 22nd St.
Oak Brook, IL 60521
(630) 472-0500

Contact:
Paul Nemecek
Email: pdncz@yahoo.com

Purpose:
To preserve and promote the culture of the Czech, Slovak and Moravian people.

Programs:
Museum, archives, exhibits, history, rare books, photos, music, art.

Website: www.czechoslovakmuseum.com

DOMINICAN AMERICAN

Dominican American Midwest Assn.
P.O. Box 3536
Oak Park, IL 60303
(708) 606-9703

Contact:
Rafael Núñez Cedeño
chair
Email: info@damamidwest.org

Purpose:
To address the needs of Dominicans and Dominican-Americans in the Midwest region. To create an avenue for analysis, planning and action concerning political, educational, economic and health-related issues that affect the lives of Dominican Americans. To create awareness in the Dominican-American community of their rights and duties in social, cultural, economic and political activity.

Programs:
Annual ball and dinner, speaking events, scholarships for students, cultural and musical events.

Website: www.damamidwest.org

DUTCH AMERICAN

Dutch Heritage Center
6601 W. College Drive
Palos Heights, IL 60463
(708) 239-4797

Contact:
G. Marcille Frederick
dir.
Jennie Huizenga
Library, Trinity Christian College
Email: marci.frederick@trnty.edu

Purpose:
To preserve the archives of Dutch accomplishments.
Programs:
Cultural preservation, education, heritage/history.

Website: http://www.trnty.edu/Library/library.html

ERITREAN AMERICAN

Association of Eritrean Community in Chicago
P.O. Box 409833
Chicago, IL 60640
(773) 593-8086

Contact:
Dr. Anghesom Atsbaha
pres.
Email: aatsbaha@gmail.com

Purpose:
To build a constructive sense of a united Eritrean community and cultural identity and to better use combined resources for a peaceful and prosperous life.
Programs:
Social, cultural, education, employment, legal advice, summer child and youth programs, heritage/history, language, literacy, translating.

ETHIOPIAN AMERICAN

Ethiopian Community Association
1730 West Greenleaf Ave.
Chicago, IL 60626
(773) 728-0303

Contact:
Erku Yimer
Email: eyimer@ecachicago.org

Purpose:
To help ease adjustment, address basic and developmental needs.
Programs:
Culture adjustment, citizenship education, counseling, employment, refugee reception and placement, health outreach, youth, entrepreneurial projects, housing, community education, translating.

Website: http://www.ecachicago.org

FILIPINO AMERICAN

Filipino American Historical Society of Chicago

5472 S. Dorchester Ave.
Chicago, IL 60615-5309
(773) 947-8696

Contact:
Estrella R. Alamar
founding pres.
Email: fahschicago@gmail.com

Purpose:
To provide a record and photographic history of Chicago's Filipino Americans; to preserve artifacts and documents; to promote public interest in the history of Chicago's Filipino Americans.

Programs:
Culture preservation, education, heritage/history, language, research, archives depository, translating.

Website: www.fahschicago.org

FINNISH AMERICAN

Finnish American Society of the Midwest and Finlandia Foundation Chapter

407 S. 6th Ave.
St. Charles, IL 60174-2935
(815) 444-4277, (630) 584-1684

Contact:
Oscar Forsman
pres.
Email: oforsman@yahoo.com, snkoivula@sbcgobal.net

Purpose:
To promote Finnish American culture, adult education and community outreach.

Programs:
Arts, workshops, lectures, adult learning, culture preservation, heritage/history, honorary consul, citizenship, legal issues, scholarships for children's language study, translation.

Website: www.fasm.us.org

GERMAN AMERICAN

American Aid Society of German Descendants

6540 N. Milwaukee Ave.
Chicago, IL 60631
Email: americansocietyofgd@gmail.com

Purpose:
Started as aid society, expanded to cultural functions.

Programs:
Children, culture preservation, heritage/history, immigrant, language, museum, senior citizen, social service, youth.

Website: http://www.americanaidsocietyofgd.org/

GERMAN AMERICAN

DANK Haus German American Cultural Center

4740 N. Western Ave.
Chicago, IL 60625
(773) 561-9181

Contact:
Nicholle Dombrowski
exec. dir.
Email: dank@dankhaus.com

Purpose:
To preserve and promote German culture, heritage, and language through activities including, maintaining a center consisting of a museum, art gallery, library and language school, and organizing educational and social programming focusing on and emphasizing the history, traditions, and contributions of Germans and German Americans.

Programs:
Kino Kaffee und Kuchen - Heimat films with cake & coffee; permanent museum exhibits, rotating fine arts exhibits ("Lost German Chicago" exhibit through Sept. 2012), cooking classes, open house, German Cinema Now, Kinderschule, adult German classes, DANKtoberfest.

Website: www.dankhaus.com

German American Chamber of Commerce of the Midwest, Inc.

321 N. Clark St., Suite 1425
Chicago, IL 60654-4714
(312) 644-2662

Contact:
Kerstin Fookin
exec. asst.
Email: Fooken@gaccom.org

Purpose:
To heighten Americans' awareness of opportunities for business in Germany and vice versa.

Programs:
Trade promotion, membership organization, database access, credit-report checks.

Website: www.gaccom.org

German American National Congress

4740 N. Western Ave.
Chicago, IL 60625
(773) 275-1100

Contact:
Eve Timmerhaus
ofc. mgr.
Email: office@dank.org

Purpose:
To cultivate German-American heritage.

Programs:
Cultural, social, German-language schools.

Website: http://www.dank.org/

GERMAN AMERICAN

German American Police Association

4740 N. Western Ave.
Chicago, IL 60625
(312) 979-5000
Email: gapabrennpunkt@aol.com

Purpose:
To provide members with functions to meet and associate with others of same heritage and job interests.
Programs:
Fraternal, charitable gifts to Altenheim Retirement.
Website: http://www.gapachicago.org

United German American Societies of Greater Chicago

6540 N. Milwaukee Avenue
Chicago IL 60631-1750
(630) 653-3018
Contact:
Helga Zettl
sec.
Email: info@germanday.com

Purpose:
To be the parent organization for approximately 60 German clubs, including social, choral, dance and educational groups.
Programs:
Culture preservation, education, heritage/history.
Website: http://www.germanday.com

GHANAIAN AMERICAN

Ghana National Council

4542 N. Broadway, Suite# 328
Chicago, IL 60640 or
P.O. Box 804787
Chicago, IL 60680-4787
(773) 636-7013 (pres.) or
(773) 388-6763
Contact:
John Henry Assabill
Email: j.assabill@att.net or
ghananationalcouncil@yahoo.com

Purpose:
To promote the general welfare and unity in the Ghanaian, African, African American and Caribbean communities in metro Chicago.
Programs:
Charitable, humanitarian, educational.
Associated organizations:
1. Asanteman Association 2. Brong-Ahafo Association
3. Ewe Association 4. Fanti Benevolent Society
5. Ga-Adangbe Community 6. Ghana Chicago Club
7. Ghana Northern Union 8. Haske Society
9. Kwahu United Association
10. Okuapeman Association
11. Okyeman Association

Website: www.ghananationalcouncil1.org/

GREEK AMERICAN

Chicago Council on Justice for Cyprus

P.O. Box 268500
Chicago, IL 60626
(630) 487-7678

Contact:
Harriette Condes-Zervakis
E-mail: HCondesZervakis@aol.com

Purpose:
To inform the public about the unresolved human rights and political issues which the people of the island Republic of Cyprus continue to face as a result of the Turkish invasion of 1974.

Programs:
Political action, informative events.

Website: http://justiceforcypruschicago.org

Greek-American Library Assn.

5026 N. Lincoln Ave.
Chicago, IL 60625
(773) 784-6662

Contact:
Aris F. Yanibas
pres.

Purpose:
To collect and preserve the books, periodicals and other materials of the entire Greek civilization, especially the Greek American experience.

Programs:
Library, lectures.

Greek Orthodox Ladies Philoptochos

40 E. Burton Place
Chicago, IL 60610
(312) 337-4130

Contact:
Joanne Stavrakas
Email: diosectary@aol.com, jojomath@aol.com

Purpose:
To be the philanthropic arm of the Greek Orthodox Church.

Programs:
Philanthropy fund, food for the hungry, scholarships, Hellenic Heart Program.

Hellenic Bar Assn. of Illinois

P.O. Box A3069
Chicago, IL 60690
(312) 243-0900

Contact:
Nick Syregelas
pres.

Purpose:
To establish and maintain the honor and dignity of the legal profession; to advance and improve the administration of justice; to protect the interests of the public, especially those of Hellenic descent; to furnish legal aid to the indigent; to advocate the equal rights of all; to cultivate social interaction among the members of the association.

Programs:
Professional support, education, legal, referral, social/fraternal, scholarships.

Website: www.members.aol.com/hbaofill

GREEK AMERICAN

Hellenic Foundation

6251-53 W. Touhy Ave.
Chicago, IL 60646
(773) 631-5222

Contact:
Teresa Colon
exec. asst.
Email: tcolon@hellenicfoundation.org

Purpose:
To be the leading professional organization in the Chicago metro Greek community; to identify and address the social service needs of individuals and families of Greek descent.

Programs:
Counseling, children, citizenship, community organizing, employment, family, housing, immigrant resettlement, literacy, referral, research, senior citizen, shelter, substance abuse, technical assistance, vocational training, youth, translating.

Website: http://www.hellenicfoundation.org/

Hellenic Family and Community Services

6251-53 W. Touhy Ave.
Chicago, IL 60646
(773) 631-5222

Contact:
Teresa Colon
Exec. asst.
Email: tcolon@hellenicfoundation.org

Purpose:
To meet the social-service needs of Greek Americans through bilingual and bicultural outreach, education, intervention and prevention.

Programs:
Counseling, children, citizenship, community organizing, education, family, immigrant resettlement and adjustment, literacy, senior citizen, substance abuse, youth, translating.

Website: http://www.hellenicfoundation.org

Hellenic Society of Constantinople

2500 N. Sheridan Road
Evanston, IL 60201
(847) 475-0044

Contact:
Jane Analitis
pres.
1885 North Braymore, Inverness IL 60010
E-mail: jnovas@comcast.net
(Jeanne Novas MD, V.P.)

Purpose:
To provide philanthropy and scholarships to related local Hellenic groups and the few remaining Orthodox Christian churches in Istanbul; to preserve our heritage; and to support the Patriarchate of the Orthodox Christians in Istanbul and religious freedom of Orthodox Christians.

Programs:
Yearly dinner dance with presentation of scholarship awards, co-sponsor Commemoration of the Fall of Constantinople, bi-annual membership meetings, occasional special events.

Website: www.hellenicsocietyconstantinople.com

GREEK AMERICAN

National Hellenic Museum
(formerly Hellenic Museum and Cultural Center)

333 S. Halsted St.
Chicago, IL 60661
(312) 655-1234

Contact:
Toula Georgakopoulos
dir. op. and prgm.
E-mail: info@hellenicmuseum.org

Purpose:
To preserve and perpetuate the heritage of the Greek culture and showcase it.

Programs:
Art exhibits and lectures, culture preservation such as archives and exhibits, children's workshops, exhibit at Children's International Fest at Navy Pier, outreach for schools education, family, heritage/history.

Website: www.nationalhellenicmuseum.org

PanHellenic Scholarship Foundation

17 N. Wabash Ave., Suite 600
Chicago, Illinois, 60602
(312) 357-6432

Contact:
Chris P. Tomaras
E-mail:
info@panhellenicscholarships.org

Purpose:
To promote education by which Greek American scholarship recipients become significant achievers and, guided by the values of their Hellenic upbringing, contribute meaningfully to the ongoing development of American society.

Programs:
Offers $250,000 in undergraduate scholarships to deserving Greek American students each year.

Website: www.panhellenicscholarships.org

United Hellenic American Congress

600 W. Jackson Suite 550
Chicago, IL 60661
(312) 775-9000

Contact:
Andrew A. Athens
chair
Email: Aathens@hellenicare.org

Purpose:
To respond to ethno-religious concerns.

Programs:
Political fundraisers, Greek heritage, cultural events, working with Greek American Parade, working with Greek Diocese to organize cultural events, lobbying, working with Hellenic Foundation on social concerns.

Website: www.hellenicare.org

GREEK AMERICAN

United Hellenic Voters of America
> 861 W. Lake St.
> Addison, IL 60101, c/o Dr. K
> (630) 628,1721

Contact:
> Dr. Dimitrios Kyriazopoulos
> *pres. and exec. dir.*

Purpose:
> To get broader representation in government.

Programs:
> Civic lectures, voter registration, translating.

Website: www.uhva.org

GUATEMALAN AMERICAN

Casa Guatemala
> 4357 N. Lincoln Ave
> Chicago, IL 60618
> (773) 407-1245
> **E-mail:** info@casaguate.org

Purpose:
> Multi-purpose.

Programs:
> Health promotion, ESL and Spanish literacy, Spanish as a Second Language, immigration information and support, Mayan culture preservation, community assistance, community organizing, human rights advocacy, youth, translating.

Website: www.casaguatemala.org

Maya Essence Fair Trade Project
> 4357 N. Lincoln Ave
> Chicago, IL 60618
> (773) 661-6947
> **E-mail:** info@mayaes.com

Purpose:
> See blog at www.mayaes.net

Programs:
> Fair Trade promotion, economic justice, eco-organic cooperatives, health promotion, community development. immigration information and support, Mayan culture preservation, community assistance, community organizing, human rights advocacy, youth, translating.

Website: www.mayessence.com

HAITIAN AMERICAN

Haitian American Community Assn.

1637 West Morse Ave
Chicago, IL 60626
(773) 956-6949

Contact:
Jacques Leblanc
pres.
E-mail: info@hacachicago.com

Purpose:
To help Haitians and Haitian-Americans make a difference by accessing social services and overcome language and cultural barriers.

Programs:
Advice on sheltering, clothing, crisis and family intervention, referral services, recreation programs for seniors, after-school program, translation and interpretation services, Food Pantry to be re-implemented soon.

Website: hacachicago.com

HISPANIC/LATINO

Alivio Medical Center

2355 S. Western Ave.
Chicago, IL 60608
(773) 254-1400

Contact:
Claudia Valenzuela
Email:
cvalenzuela@aliviomedicalcenter.org

Purpose:
To provide bilingual and bicultural health care and health education for the uninsured and under-insured.

Programs:
Health services, advocacy, education, research, evaluation.

Website: http://www.aliviomedicalcenter.org

Aspira

2415 N. Milwaukee Ave.
Chicago, Ill. 60647
(773) 252-0970

Contact:
Carline Murillo
Email: info@aspirail.org,
cmurillo@aspirail.org

Purpose:
To develop leadership skills of Latino youth.

Programs:
Leadership Development Institute, health careers, drug prevention, Aspira Parents for Educational Excellence, math and science, alternative high school, college counseling, financial aid, heritage/history, wliteracy, mentoring, tutoring, translating.

Website: www.aspirail.org

HISPANIC/LATINO

CALOR, a Division of Anixter Center

5038 W. Armitage Ave.
Chicago, IL 60639
(773) 385-9080

Contact:
Rosa E. Martínez Colón, M.S.
asst. dir.
Email: remartinez-colon@anixter.org;
askcalor@anixter.org

Purpose:
To provide holistic planning and coordination of health services to Latinos at risk for or living with HIV/AIDS and/or other disabilities, to empower them to live and work in the community.

Programs:
Case management, employment services, housing, prevention and education, referrals, HIV/STI testing.

Website: www.calor.org

Casa Aztlan

1831 S. Racine
Chicago, IL 60608
(312) 666-5509 ext. 122

Contact:
Carlos Arango
Email: carlos@casaaztlan.org

Purpose:
To support heritage and culture; to offer assistance to underprivileged Latinos.

Programs:
Arts, counseling, citizenship, education, literacy, community center, youth after-school, translating.

Website: http://www.casaaztlan.org

Casa Central

1343 N. California Ave.
Chicago, IL 60622
(773) 645-2300

Contact:
Ann Alvarez
pres. & CEO
Email: fdiaz@casacentral.org
(Frank Diaz, mktg. assoc.)

Purpose:
To transform lives and strengthen communities, using our network of 25 social service programs to help children, individuals, families and seniors become self-sufficient.

Programs:
Preschool (Head Start) and after-school programs, violence prevention and counseling, pre-employment training, Certified Nursing Assistant training, adult daycare, child welfare, foster grandparents, home-based care and assistance, nutrition, transitional housing for homeless families, and community-based access to computers.
Additional locations: 1335 N. California, 1349 N. California, 2222 N. Kedzie

Website: www.casacentral.org

HISPANIC/LATINO

Centro de Información
28 N. Grove Ave., Suite 200
Elgin, IL 60120
(847) 695-9050
Contact:
Cheryl Wilkins
asst. dir.
Email:
c.wilkins@centrodeinformacion.org

Purpose:
To empower Hispanics with the ability to effectively integrate into the greater community through the facilitation of information, education, and citizenship.

Programs:
Counseling, citizenship and immigration, employment, mental health, information and referral, public benefits, after-school homework assistance, parenting skills training, life skills seminars, programs for at-risk families, emergency food pantry.
Other offices: 2380 Glendale Terr. #8, Hanover Park, IL 60103 and 150 S. Kennedy Dr., Suite 8-B, Carpentersville, IL 60110

Website: www.centrodeinformacion.org

Centro Romero
6216 N. Clark St.
Chicago, IL 60660
(773) 508-5300
Contact:
Daysi Funes
exec. dir.
Email: info@centroromero.org

Purpose:
Multi-service community center for economically and educationally disadvantaged.

Programs:
Adult education (ESL, citizenship, Spanish GED), domestic violence counseling, youth programs, legal (immigration), family services (public benefits applications and referrals).

Website: www.centroromero.org

Centro Sin Frontera
2716 W. Division St.
Chicago, IL 60622
(773) 847-7282
Contact:
Emma Lozana
pres.
Email: psf@somosunpueblo.com

Purpose:
To educate and mobilize to bring needed services to improve the quality of life in our community.

Programs:
Citizenship classes, workshop on immigrant rights, health-education classes, WIC, housing, legal clinic, education committees with block-by-block structure.

Website: www.familialatinaunida.org

HISPANIC/LATINO

Chicago Religious Leadership Network on Latin America

4750 N. Sheridan Rd., Suite 429
Chicago, IL 60640
(773) 293-2964 and -3680

Contact:
Jim Vondracek
mng. dir.
Email: crln@crln.org

Purpose:
To provide educational opportunities about Latin America (mainly Central America, Cuba and Mexico) through delegations and speaking events; to advocate for just U.S. policies toward Latin America.

Programs:
Speakers regarding human rights, economics, political atmosphere of a specific country, delegations to Latin America, lobbying in Washington, D.C.

Website: www.crln.org

East Village Youth Program

3643 W. Belmont Ave.
Chicago, IL 60618
(312) 275-0440

Contact:
Sarah Bird
Email: outreach1@evyp.org

Purpose:
The mission of East Village Youth Program is to encourage and prepare primarily low-income, Latino youth for a college education. EVYP further strives to support these youth as they pursue their college degrees and enter professional careers.

Programs:
College readiness program, including academic preparation, skill-building, service-learning, college visits, tutoring.

Website: www.evyp.org

Hispanic Alliance for Career Enhancement (HACE)

100 S. Wacker Dr, Suite 700
Chicago, IL 60606
(312) 435-0498

Contact:
Mario Vela, M.S.
dir.
Email: mario@haceonline.org

Purpose:
To empower Hispanics to occupy economic leadership positions, thus benefiting Hispanic community.

Programs:
Employer Support Program, annual career conference, career development seminars.

Website: http://www.haceonline.org/

HISPANIC/LATINO

Hispanic American Construction Industry Association

901 W. Jackson Blvd., Suite 205
Chicago, IL 60607
(312) 666-5910

Contact:
Jorge Perez
exec. dir.
Email: info@haciaworks.org

Purpose:
To advocate on behalf of minority- and women-owned businesses and ensure equitable participation of its members in the Chicago area construction industry; to promote growth, professionalism, integrity and quality of work.

Programs:
Economic development, business support, membership services such as contract opportunities and referral, marketing assistance, MBE certification assistance, business workshops, conflict resolution assistance.

Website: www.haciaworks.org

Hispanic Housing Development Corp.

325 N. Wells Street, 8th Floor
Chicago, IL 60654
(312) 602-6500

Contact:
Patty Bonta
ofc. mgr.
Email: pbonta@hhdevcorp.com

Programs:
To provide quality, affordable housing for Latino neighborhoods and encourage economic development.

Purpose:
Quality affordable housing for low-moderate income residents, serving elderly, disabled, multi-family and single occupancies; assistance with referrals to community agencies.

Website: www.hhdc.org

Hispanocare, Inc.

836 W. Wellington
Chicago, IL 60657
(773) 296-7157

Contact:
Daniel Maldonado
mkting & outreach
Email: Daniel.maldonado@advocatehealth.com

Purpose:
To provide quality, user-friendly, culturally sensitive health care to Hispanics.

Programs:
Health care, education.

Website: www.hispanocare.org

HISPANIC/LATINO

Illinois Association of Hispanic State Employees

P.O. Box 641526
Chicago, IL 60664-1526
(312) 814-8942

Contact:
Martha Lopez
Email: iahse.assoc@illinois.gov

Purpose:
To increase Hispanic employment at the state level and develop services to help the Hispanic community and Hispanics in government.

Programs:
Educational yearly conference for state employees and state university employees; workshops on communication skills; career development; monthly meetings.

Website: www.iahse.org

Illinois Migrant Council

28 E. Jackson Blvd. #1600
Chicago, IL 60604
(312) 663-1522

Contact:
Eloy Salazar
exec. dir.
Email: info@illinoismigrant.org

Purpose:
To provide employment, education and other opportunities for migrant and seasonal farmworkers and others who face obstacles to attaining economic self-sufficiency in rural Illinois.

Programs:
Job training and placement, adult education, health prevention education, family literacy, social services, crisis intervention, technology learning, outreach and referrals.

Website: www.illinoismigrant.org

Illinois Migrant Legal Assistance Project (IMLAP)

111 West Jackson Blvd., Ste. 300
Chicago, IL 60604
(312) 423-5902

Contact:
Miguel Keberlein Gutiérrez
Email: mkeberlein@lafchicago.org

Purpose:
To provide legal assistance to migrant workers.

Programs:
Legal services.

Website: www.lafchicago.org

HISPANIC/LATINO

Instituto del Progreso Latino

2570 S. Blue Island Ave.
Chicago, IL 60608
(773) 890-0055

Contact:
Yvonne Nieves
Email: y.nieves@idpl.org

Purpose:
To provide better educational services to the community.
Programs:
Primarily educational; some social services, immigrant, advocacy.
Website: http://www.idpl.org/

International Latino Cultural Center

676 N. LaSalle St. Suite 520
Chicago, IL 60611
(312) 431-1330

Contact:
Pepe Vargas
Email: info@latinoculturalcenter.com

Purpose:
To promote Latino culture and create greater awareness of Latinos' contributions.
Programs:
Arts, heritage/history, children, education, Chicago Latino Film Festival, translating.
Website: www.ChicagoLatinoFilmFestival.org

Latin American Chamber of Commerce

3512 W. Fullerton Ave.
Chicago, IL 60647
(773) 252-5211

Contact:
German Larrea
Email:
glarrea@latinamericanchamberofcommerce.com

Purpose:
To organize all Hispanic businesses as one economic group; to foster growth and development among members by providing professional and technical assistance and management education/training; to facilitate business transactions between members; to increase level of employment of local residents through entrepreneurship.
Programs:
Financial consulting, government contracting, business insurance, general business consulting.
Website: http://latinamericanchamberofcommerce.com/

HISPANIC/LATINO

Latin American Police Association

Contact:
Michael J. Chuchro
pres.
Email: Info@lapa1961.com
president@lapa1961.com

Purpose:
To develop, promote and encourage a greater degree of understanding and cooperation between the Hispanic community and local, state and federal law enforcement agencies; to promote a higher degree of professionalism, education and advancement among Hispanic law enforcement officers. LAPA has evolved into an issue-oriented organization that seeks to enhance the quality of life for both Hispanic law enforcement officers and for the Hispanic communities we serve.

Programs:
Networking and education. Founded Hispanic Institute of Law Enforcement. Annual Awards Recognition Banquet, golf outing, comedy show, summer cruise, and Family Christmas Party.

Website: www.LAPA1961.com

Latin United Community Housing Association

3541 W. North Ave.
Chicago, IL 60647
(773) 276-5338

Contact:
Eli Barbosa
Email: ebarbosa@lucha.org

Purpose:
To provide decent and affordable housing, housing services and education to low- and moderate-income Latinos and other residents. LUCHA fosters community stability in neighborhoods lacking adequate housing due to discrimination on the basis of race, national origin, religion, familial status, and disability.

Programs:
Empowering residents through education and participation, promoting affordable housing development and home ownership, rehabilitating and managing housing, providing organizing leadership and advocating for resources. (LUCHA is a HUD certified housing counseling agency.)

Website: www.lucha.org

HISPANIC/LATINO

Latino Counseling Service
(Counseling Center of Lake View)
3225 N. Sheffield
Chicago, IL 60657
(773) 549-5886

Contact:
Astrid Hesse, PsyD
Email: ahesse@cclakeview.org

Purpose:
To provide for mental health needs of Spanish-speaking population.

Programs:
Individual, family and group counseling of adults, children and adolescents, family violence, substance abuse, and immigration services.

Website: www.cclakeview.org

Latino Policy Forum
180 N. Michigan Ave., Suite 1250
Chicago, IL 60601
(312) 376-1766

Contact:
Sylvia Puente
exec. dir.
Email: info@additopolicyforum.org

Purpose:
To build the power, influence, and leadership of the Latino community through collective action to transform public policies that ensure the well being of our community and society as a whole.

Programs:
Community engagement and capacity building, early childhood education, housing issues that address affordability, accessibility and equity, and immigration reform and immigrant integration.

Website: www.latinopolicyforum.org

Latino Progresando
3047 W. Cermak Road
Chicago, IL 60623
(773) 542-7077

Contact:
Luis Gutierrez
exec. dir.

Purpose:
To serve immigrants with the highest quality low-cost legal immigration services, community education/engagement and advocacy organizing around policy that affects immigrants.

Programs:
Access to justice, arts and education, youth advancement.

Website: www.latinospro.org

HISPANIC/LATINO

Latino Treatment Center

2608 W. Peterson Ave.
Chicago, IL 60659
(773) 465-1161

Contact:
Adrina Trino

Purpose:
Provide alcohol/drug treatment to underserved Hispanic population.

Programs:
Alcohol and drug treatment.
Other facilities: Latino Treatment Center in Elgin and West Chicago (see immediately below)

Website: www.latinotreatmentcenter.com

Latino Treatment Center - Elgin

54 S. Grove Ave.
Elgin, IL 60120
(847) 695-9155

Contact:
Adriana Trino
Email: adri1631@aol.com

Purpose:
To help the Latino population.

Programs:
DUI evaluation and individual counseling; DUI remedial education with group and family counseling, DUI risk intervention program and adolescent treatment, outpatient treatment for dual diagnosis and chemical dependency problems, translating.
Other offices: 2608 W. Peterson Ave., Chicago, IL 60659 (773) 465-1161,
245 W. Roosevelt Rd., West Chicago IL, 60185 (630) 293-9707

Little Village Chamber of Commerce

3610 W. 26th St., 2nd floor
Chicago, IL 60623
(773) 521-5387

Contact:
Nilda Esparza
exec. dir.
E-mail: nilda@lavillitachamber.org

Purpose:
Economic development.

Programs:
Training, assistance, advocacy, community development.

Website: www.lavillitachamber.org

HISPANIC/LATINO

Little Village Community Council

3610 W. 26th Street
Chicago, IL 60623
(312) 286-3405

Contact:
August Sallas
pres.
E-mail: sallas@sbcglobal.net

Purpose:
To organize and empower the Mexican community in Little Village.

Programs:
Free haircuts & manicures, free movies, food pantry, free clothes, Back to School block party, Museum of Mexican Culture & History, Senior Citizens club, city and state resources, health fair, legal clinic, English classes, voter registration, Chicago Public Schools Local School Council workshops.

Website: http://lvcc.web.officelive.com

Mexican American Legal Defense & Education Fund (MALDEF)

11 East Adams Street, Suite 700
Chicago, IL 60603
(312) 427-0701

Contact:
Alonzo Rivas
regional counsel
E-mail: rsantos@maldef.org

Purpose:
To protect the civil rights of Latinos.

Programs:
Class-action cases in areas of education, voting rights, immigration, employment discrimination.

Website: www.maldef.org

Mexican Civic Society of Illinois, Inc.

3760 W. 38th St.
Chicago, IL 60632
(773) 376-8445

Contact:
Evelia Rodriguez
V.P. and gen. coord.
Email:
info@sociedadcivicamexicana.org

Purpose:
To preserve culture and traditions.

Programs:
Organize main Mexican Parade in downtown Chicago, civic ceremony of "El Grito" at Millennium Park, celebrate other important dates in Mexico's history, Day of the Mexican Flag, Benito Juarez, Cinco de Mayo, Queen Election, Aztec Gala Banquet, Revolution Day, scholarships.

Website: www.sociedadcivicamexicana.org

HISPANIC/LATINO

Mujeres Latinas En Accion
(Latin Women in Action)
2124 W. 21st Place
Chicago, IL 60608
(773) 890-7676
Email: mujeresmail@mujereslat.org

Purpose:
To serve monolingual Spanish-speaking women; to advocate for linguistically and culturally sensitive services in all areas, including courts, police and social service agencies.

Programs:
Domestic violence and sexual-assault prevention and counseling, Latina leadership training, homelessness prevention, parent support groups, after-school tutoring and recreation for children 5-12, youth crisis intervention.

Website: www.mujereslatinasenaccion.org

National Council of La Raza, Midwest Regional Office
303 W. Erie St., Suite 310
Chicago, IL 60654
(312) 269-9250

Purpose:
To empower Hispanics, from the grassroots up, and build a community-based constituency predicated on mutual respect and credibility.

Programs:
Advocacy, assistance in management, program operations and resource development for community-based organizations; applied research and policy analysis; public information; special and international projects.

Website: www.nclr.org

National Museum of Mexican Art
(previously Mexican Fine Arts Center)
1852 W. 19th St.
Chicago, IL 60608
(312) 738-1503

Contact:
Carlos Tortolero
exec. dir.

Email:
info@nationalmuseumofmexicanart.org

Purpose:
To preserve and promote the cultural/artistic expression of the Mexican culture in and outside of Mexico.

Programs:
Cultural center/museum, events and exhibits, permanent collection of Mexican art, professional development of local Mexican artists, arts education, advocacy.

Website: http://www.nationalmuseumofmexicanart.org/

HISPANIC/LATINO

Pilsen Neighbors Community Council

2026 S. Blue Island
Chicago, IL 60608
(312) 666-2663

Contact:
Juan F. Soto
Email: jfsoto@gamaliel.org

Purpose:
To develop effective leaders in the community.

Programs:
Leadership development.

Website: pilsenneighbors.org

The Resurrection Project

1818 S. Paulina St.
Chicago, IL 60608
(312) 666-1323

Contact:
Vauna Hernandez
HR mgr.
Email: info@resurrectionproject.org

Purpose:
To build relationships and challenge people to act on their faith and values to create healthy communities through organizing, education and community development.

Programs:
Community organizing and development, economic development, housing, family.

Website: www.resurrectionproject.org

Segundo Ruiz Belvis Cultural Center

4046 W. Armitage
Chicago, IL 60647
(773) 698-6004

Contact:
Arnaldo Cruz
Email: arnaldo.cruz@segundoruizbelvis.org

Purpose:
To offer community empowerment, revitalization through culture, and other self-development services.

Programs:
Counseling, art, cultural, music, dance, GED classes, literacy, ESL.

Website: http://www.srbcc.org

Spanish Action Committee of Chicago

2452 W. Division St.
Chicago, IL, 60622
(773) 292-1052

Contact:
Leoncio Vazquez
pres. & CEO
Email: mail@spanishaction.com

Purpose:
To meet the educational, cultural, social and economic needs of the community.

Programs:
Low Income Home Energy Assistance Program (LIHEAP); referrals for shelter, ESL and GED programs; legal assistance; food programs, employment and housing; voter registration and education; and Energy Action Network (EAN) site.

Website: www.spanishaction.com

HISPANIC/LATINO

The United Neighborhood Organization of Chicago (UNO)

954 W. Washington Blvd., 3rd floor
Chicago, IL 60607
(312) 432-6301

Contact:
Juan Rangel
CEO
Email: wmejia@uno-online.org

Purpose:
To challenge Hispanics to attain standards of excellence toward an overall enfrancisement of the community, both in a broad sense of American social growth and at the local level in terms of stable neighborhoods and healthy families.

Programs:
Education, economic development, citizenship, leadership, advocacy.

Website: www.uno-online.org

Westtown Concerned Citizens Coalition

3501 W. Armitage Ave.
Chicago, IL 60647
(773) 235-2144

Contact:
Tito Vargas
exec. dir.
Email: westtowncoalition@yahoo.com

Purpose:
Provide needed community services.

Programs:
Crime, drug and gang prevention; workshops and seminars for youth, parents; economic development, housing, adult education GED, ESL, citizenship, advocacy, immigrant counseling, referral, translating.

(See also Guatemalan, Puerto Rican)

INDIAN AMERICAN

Alliance of Midwest Indian Associations

642 N. Ashbury Ave.
Bolingbrook, IL 60440-1164
(630) 739-7089

Contact:
Prem Lalvani
Email: aaccmarch1@aol.com

Purpose:
To promote good will and welfare of the society and lead our community to participate in the affairs of mainstream America; to provide services to the society we live in while enhancing Indo-American identity and developing understanding and closer ties with others.

Programs:
Indian Republic Day celebration, Asian American Coalition banquet, health fair, India Day parade, Thanksgiving dinner open to all, assistance for discrimination on the job and in the community.

INDIAN AMERICAN

American Association of Physicians from India

600 Enterprise Drive, Suite 108
Oak Brook, IL 60523
(630) 990-2277
Email: info@aapiusa.org

Contact:
Sunita Kanumury, MD
pres.

Purpose:
To facilitate and enable Indian American physicians to excel in patient care, teaching and research and to pursue their aspirations in professional and community affairs.

Programs:
Patient care, teaching, research, advocacy.

Website: www.aapiusa.org

Association of Rajasthanis in America

2S711 Avenue Latour
Oak Brook, IL 60523
(630) 853-2946

Purpose:
To promote the spiritual and cultural growth of Rajasthani Americans and to preserve the traditions and heritage of Rajasthan among all Rajasthani generations.

Programs:
Three annual functions: Holi, Diwali and summertime picnic.

Website: http://www.chicagoara.org/

Federation of Indo American Christians of Greater Chicago

410 Potter Rd.
Des Plaines, IL 60016
(847) 296-3803

Contact:
Dr. Jayachand Pallekonda
Email: info@fiacona.org

Purpose:
To serve the community needs of the Indo American Christians in Illinois.

Programs:
Fund raising for the needy, particularly in a natural disaster, general assistance, support services, community organizing, cultural/music, translating.

Website: http://fiacona.org/

INDIAN AMERICAN

Federation of India Assn.
850 East Higgins Road
Schaumburg, IL 60173
(847) 517-8640

Contact:
Sunil Shah
pres.

Purpose:
Umbrella organization of other Indian associations in the Chicago area and Midwest, representing more than 150,00 Indian Americans.

Programs:
Celebrates Indian events such as India Republic Day, India Independence Day, Diwali Day, Garbha Festival.

Website: http://www.fia-il.com/

Gujarat Cultural Assn.
807 Cardinal Lane
Elk Grove Village, Chicago, IL 60007
(847) 524-7296

Purpose:
To bring together the Gujarati community in Chicago and preserve the heritage through cultural events.

Programs:
Dinners, dance shows, New Year's celebrations.

India Development Service
P.O. Box 980
Chicago, IL 60690
(708) 524-2041

Contact:
Jagjit Jain
Email: Jagjitj@gmail.com

Purpose:
To aid social/economic development of disadvantaged people.

Programs:
Economic development, education, health care, literacy, vocational training, women.

Website: www.idsusa.org

Indo-American Center
6328 N. California Ave.
Chicago, IL 60659
(773) 973-4444

Contact:
Jay Luthra
exec. dir.
Email: info@indoamerican.org

Purpose:
To help South Asian immigrants in the Chicago area become empowered and connected through education, resources, and social services.

Programs:
Citizenship and immigration services, adult literacy (ESL), seniors, civics education, public benefits assistance, youth, computer, and Cyriac D. Kappil Legal Clinic.

Website: www.indoamerican.org

INDIAN AMERICAN

Punjabi Cultural Society of Chicago
P. O. Box 1244
Palatine, IL 60078
(847) 359-5727
Email: info@PCSChicago.org

Purpose:
To promote education, good citizenship, Punjabi culture, language, performing arts, healthy life style, and sports in the metropolitan Chicago area.

Programs:
Dance competitions, cultural shows, scholarships for Punjabi students, sports nights.

Website: http://www.pcschicago.org/aa/

IRANIAN AMERICAN

Pasfarda Art & Cultural Exchange
1800 W. Roscoe Ave. Suite 233
Chicago, IL 60657
Contact:
Avisheh Mohsenin
pres.
Email: contact@pasfarda.org

Purpose:
To strengthen cultural understanding between Iranians and Americans to create innovative alliances, coalitions and affiliations.

Programs:
Exhibitions, screenings and performances for Iranian artists and intellectuals, dialogue, education and artistic exchange.

Website: www.pasfarda.org

IRAQI AMERICAN

Iraqi Mutual Aid Society

6328 N. Clark St., Suite 1
Chicago, IL 60660
(773) 956-4727, (773) 290-9192

Contact:
Anass Al Bayati
dir. pgm. admin.

Email:
anass.albayati@iraqimutualaid.org,
info@iraqimutualaid.org

Purpose:
Non-profit organization assisting refugees, easing transition, building community, preserving culture.

Programs:
Orientation, cultural adaptations, support for new arrivals, employment and career, English as Second Language (ESL) by Arabic teacher, Arabic classes for kids.

Website: http://iraqimutualaid.weebly.com/

IRISH AMERICAN

Irish American Alliance

11134 S. Western Ave.
Chicago, IL 60655
(773) 233-5040, 229-8800

Contact:
Thomas Lynch
secy.

Purpose:
To provide social and charitable activities and to establish a retirement home.

Programs:
Social, charitable, heritage/history, culture, job network, scholarship program.

Website: www.chicagoiaa.org

Irish American Heritage Center

4626 N. Knox Ave.
Chicago, IL 60630
(773) 282-7035

Contact:
Tim McDonnell
exec. dir.

Email: info@irishahc.org

Purpose:
To promote and preserve the Irish culture, language and arts.

Programs:
Arts, culture, dance, music, theater, museum, social activities, children, seniors' groups, language classes, immigration assistance, genealogy, library, banquet rentals and a full-service pub.

Website: www.irish-ameerican.org

ITALIAN AMERICAN

Amerital Unico Club of Chicago

2003 W. Grand Ave.
Chicago, IL 60612
(312) 829-2460

Contact:
Anthony J. Fornelli
Email: ajf@comcast.net

Purpose:
To foster community awareness and to provide a positive attitude toward Italian Americans.

Programs:
Involved with the Italian American Veterans Museum and Library, which houses artifacts, weaponry, uniforms displaying the role of Italian Americans in all the wars of this nation from Revolutionary time.

Columbian Club of Chicago

c/o Anthony J. Morizzo
7 Westlake Drive
South Barrington, IL 60010
(847) 417-5738

Contact:
Anthony Morizzo
Email: 1946mraj@comcast.net

Purpose:
To provide a variety of social, business and charitable events.

Programs:
Civic welfare, social, business and professional standards, preservation of Italian ethnicity.

Italian American Chamber of Commerce

500 N. Michigan Ave, Suite 506
Chicago, IL., 60611
(312) 553-9137

Contact:
Fulvio Calcinardi
Email: info@iacc-chicago.com

Purpose:
Support the Italian American professional community, network its members and mobilize business activity.

Programs:
Networking events, industry events, trade missions, Italian Expo, annual gala and awards dinner, golf outing, bocce tournament, fundraising.

Website: www.iacc-chicago.com

Italian American Labor Council

(312) 485-3100

Contact:
Mike Fdanzo
Email: lalc2009@aol.com

Purpose:
To provide activities that are charitable, benevolent, civic, educational, patriotic and social.

Programs:
Citizenship, culture preservation, education, charitable, heritage/history, social.

Website: http://www.chicagoialc.com/

52

ITALIAN AMERICAN

Italian-American Police Association

6351 W. Montrose, Suite 210
Chicago, IL 60634-1563
(312) 415-1202

Contact:
Anthony Langone
pres.
Email: iapavp@aol.com

Purpose:
To carry out an educational program to improve the administration of justice; to cultivate talents in suitable candidates for various governmental law agencies.

Programs:
Training seminars, legislative alerts, fraternal cooperation, national/ethnic pride.

Website: www.iapa-il.org

Italian Cultural Center at Casa Italia

3800 W. Division St.
Stone Park, 60165
(708) 345-5933

Contact:
Tony Turano
chr.
Email: info@casaitaliachicago.org

Purpose:
To pursue common goals, preserve our past, celebrate our heritage and ensure passage of values to future generations.

Programs:
Arts, counseling, children, culture preservation, heritage/history, vocal scholarships, religious program, Italian classes, social services, translating.

Website: www.casaitaliachicago.org

Joint Civic Committee of Italian Americans

3800 Division St.,
Stone Park, Illinois 60165
(708) 450-9050

Contact:
Jo Ann Serpico
exec. dir.
Email: jcc@jccia.com

Purpose:
To preserve Italian American culture and provide a unified voice for Chicago's Italian American community.

Programs:
Civic and cultural events such as Columbus Day parade, Italian Heritage Ball and Cotillion, Cardinal Bernadin Humanitarian of the Year Award, Dante Award to a member of the media, scholarships, fights against defamation and discrimination.

Website: www.jccia.com

ITALIAN AMERICAN

Justinian Society of Lawyers

734 North Wells St.
Chicago, IL 60654
(708) 441-4119

Contact:
Nina Albano Vidmer
Email: justinians@navandassoc.com

Purpose:
To promote the exchange of ideas and the advancement of legal issues among attorneys and judges of Italian descent.

Programs:
Monthly dinner meetings with speakers, scholarships, golf outing, Christmas dinner dance.

Website: www.justinians.org

National Italian American Sports Hall of Fame

1431 Taylor St.
Chicago, IL 60607
(312) 226-5566

Contact:
Sam Tornatore
pres.

Purpose:
To raise money for scholar athletes and honor Italian American athletes.

Programs:
Civic, educational, philanthropic, heritage/history.

Website: www.niashf.org

Order of Sons of Italy in America

Grand Lodge, State of Illinois
9447 W. 144th Place
Orland Park, IL 60462
(708) 403-7822

Contact:
Valerie Ozzanto-Wanda
ofc. mgr.
Email: osiail@aol.com

Purpose:
To preserve cultural heritage, promote the positive contributions of Italian Americans, encourage participation in the political and civic life of our communities and raise money for national and international charities and scholarships.

Programs:
Social/fraternal, culture preservation, scholarships, charity.

St. Anthony Chapter 13 IANU

8300 W. Lawrence
Norridge, IL 60656
(708) 456-8300

Contact:
Anthony Lupo
founder

Purpose:
To provide charity and scholarships.

Programs:
Fund raising for charities, holiday food baskets for the needy, scholarships.

ITALIAN AMERICAN

Society S.S. Crocifisso

706 E. Ivy Lane
Arlington Heights, IL 60004
(847) 577-8230

Contact:
Frank Faraci
pres.
Email: info@sscrocifisso.us

Purpose:
To promote and maintain the religious welfare of the Italian community in Chicago.

Programs:
Annual feast of Santissimo Crocifisso di Ciminna in Chicago held on the second weekend in June on the grounds of Maryville Academy in Des Plaines; annual dinner dance in the fall.

Website: www.sscrocifisso.us

Unico National, Greater Chicago Chapter

Illinois District One
1621 N. 76th Court
Elmwood Park, IL 60707
(708) 452-9070

Contact:
Edward R. Gesualdo
dist. gov.

Purpose:
To raise funds for charitable organizations.

Programs:
Philanthropic.

Unico National

Chicago Amerital Chapter
8770 W. Bryn Mawr, Suite 1200
Chicago, IL 60631
(773) 380-8300

Contact:
Adam Paoli
pres.
Email: paoli.adam@gmail.com

Purpose:
To raise funds for charitable organizations.

Programs:
Philanthropic.

Unico National

Chicago West Suburban Chapter
1834 North 74th Ave.
Elmwood Park, IL 60707
(708) 655-5340, (773) 384-9513

Contact:
William Randazzo
pres.

Purpose:
To raise funds for charitable organizations.

Programs:
Philanthropic.

ITALIAN AMERICAN

Unico National
Chicago South
220 Prairieview Dr.
Palos Park, IL 60464
Contact:
James Purrazzo
pres.
Email: purrazzo@ameritech.net

Purpose:
To raise funds for charitable organizations.
Programs:
Philanthropic.

Veneti Del Nord America
613 W. Eggerding Dr.
Addison, IL 60101
(630) 628-5177
Contact:
Attilio Scolaro
pres.

Purpose:
To keep close ties with the culture and provide a bridge between new and old generations to instill their culture and tradition.
Programs:
Work with Italian Cultural Center, helping with banquets, selling tickets; charity work helping Veneti families in time of need.

JAPANESE AMERICAN

Chicago Japanese American Citizens League
5415 N. Clark St.
Chicago, IL 60640
(773) 728-7170
Contact:
William (Bill) Yoshino
Midwest dir.
Email: midwest@jacl.org

Purpose:
To protect the welfare of the Japanese American/Asian American community.
Programs:
Civil rights, cultural preservation, education, leadership development.

JAPANESE AMERICAN

Chicago Japanese American Historical Society

745 Beaver Rd.
Glenview, IL 60025
(847) 998-8101

Contact:
Jean Mishima
pres.
Email: jmmishima@hotmail.com

Purpose:
To educate the general public of the Japanese American experiences and document and preserve Japanese American history.

Programs:
First voice-presentation of the Japanese American experiences of pre-, during, and post-WWII; education, heritage/history, research.

Website: www.cjahs.org

Japanese American Service Committee of Chicago

4427 North Clark St.
Chicago, IL 60640
(773) 275-7212

Contact:
Susan Tybon
CEO
Email: jascinfo@jasc-chicago.org

Purpose:
To meet the social and cultural needs of Japanese Americans in the Chicago area.

Programs:
Counseling, adult day care, health care, home help, cultural, arts & crafts, nutrition.

Website: www.jasc-chicago.org

Japanese Mutual Aid Society of Chicago

2249 W. Berwyn Ave.
Chicago, IL 60625-1118
(773) 907-3002

Contact:
Karen Kanemoto

Purpose:
To serve those Japanese Americans interested in being laid to rest among other members of their culture

Programs:
Memoiral Day services, final rites and burial for destitute, location of Japanese relatives of deceased.

JEWISH AMERICAN

American-Israel Chamber of Commerce of Metropolitan Chicago, Inc.

500 Lake Cook Road, Suite 350
Deerfield, IL 60015
(847) 597-7069

Contact:
Michael R. Schmitt
exec. dir.
Email: m.schmitt@americaisrael.org

Purpose:
To develop mutually beneficial and profitable commercial relationships between U.S. and Israeli firms.

Programs:
Trade, economic development, business exchanges.

American Jewish Committee

55 E. Monroe, Suite 2930
Chicago, IL 60603
(312) 251-8800

Contact:
Daniel E. Elbaum
exec. dir.
Email: Chicago@ajc.org

Purpose:
To secure the religious and civil rights of Jews and all groups; to encourage support for Israel; to work toward strengthening the vitality of the Jewish community.

Programs:
Inter-ethnic, inter-racial and inter-religious dialogues; prejudice-reduction programs for high schools; political advocacy; educational programs.

Anti-Defamation League

120 S. LaSalle St., Suite 1150
Chicago, IL 60603
(312) 553-3939

Contact:
David Kurzmann
asst. dir.
Greater Chicago/Upper Midwest
Email: chiadl@adl.org

Purpose:
To combat anti-Semitism and all forms of hatred, prejudice and bigotry.

Programs:
Advocacy, education, civil rights and human relations.

JEWISH AMERICAN

Association of Reform Zionists of America (ARZA)

Central District office
555 Skokie Blvd., Ste. 333
Northbrook, IL 60062
(847) 239-6974

Contact:
Marlene Dodinval
Central Dist. dir.
Email: mdodinval@arza.org

Purpose:
To develop support for and strengthen the Reform movement in Israel and promote advocacy for a pluralistic, just and democratic society in the State of Israel.

Programs:
Philanthropic activities in support of the Israeli Reform movement and its institutions; speakers, advocacy programs.

Website: www.ARZA.org

The Ark

6450 N. California
Chicago, IL 60645
(773) 973-1000

Contact:
Miriam Weinberger
Email: ark@arkchicago.org

Purpose:
To serve the indigent in the target population (mostly Jewish Americans in Chicago and suburbs).

Programs:
Food pantry, counseling, medical, legal, social, translating.

Website: www.arkchicago.org

B'nai B'rith, Region 11

143 North LaSalle St., Suite 1530
Chicago, IL 60602
(312) 551-0011

Contact:
Cary Wolovick
program coord.
Email: bbrith@sbcglobal.net

Purpose:
To be the global voice of Jewish community, to provide a platform for Jewish communal concerns.

Programs:
Senior housing, Jewish education, culture preservation, community services, interfaith dialogues, promotion of democracy and world peace, UN advocacy.

Website: www.bnaibrith.org/regions_and_communities/midwest.cfm

JEWISH AMERICAN

BBYO Inc.
(B'nai B'rith Youth Organization)

300 Revere Drive
Northbrook, IL 60062
(224) 406-9261
E-mail: gmr@bbyo.org

Contact:
Stacy Heller
sr. program dir.

Purpose:
To develop leadership skills, build self-esteem and work toward a stronger Jewish community.

Programs:
Leadership training, social, recreational, community service.

Website: www.gmrbbyo.org

CJE SeniorLife

3003 W. Touhy
Chicago, IL 60645
(773) 508-1000

Contact:
Mark D. Weiner
pres. & CEO (773)508-1005
Email: info@cje.net

Purpose:
Comprehensive network of community-based and residential programs in order to enhance the lives of seniors.

Programs:
Home-delivered meals, transportation, adult day services, counseling, geriatric care management, consumer assistance, home health, personal care, subsidized and affordable independent living apartments, skilled nursing (including Alzheimer's care) and short-term rehabilitation, healthy living programming, health and wellness check-ups and education, support groups. Other locations: Lieberman Center for Health and Rehabilitation in Skokie; CJE Adult Day Services in Evanston, Deerfield and Chicago; Weinberg Community for Senior Living in Deerfield, affordable apartments in 6 locations throughout metro Chicago; Robineau Residence group living in Skokie.

Website: www.cje.net

JEWISH AMERICAN

Decalogue Society of Lawyers

39 S. LaSalle St., Suite 410
Chicago, IL 60603
(312) 263-6493

Contact:
Aviva Patt
Email: decaloguesociety@gmail.com

Purpose:
To combine the attributes of members' lives as attorneys and Jews to accomplish public service and social action, using the activities, goals and strengths of a bar association.

Programs:
Free legal lecture series open to public; human rights, civil rights, culture preservation, financial aid, community building with other ethnic and non-ethnic bar associations; student involvement; jobs board; networking; social events; awards programs; judicial evaluation.

Website: http://decaloguesociety.org

EZRA Multi-Service Center

909 W. Wilson Ave.
Chicago, IL 60640
(773) 275-0866

Contact:
Anita Weinstein
Email: cnovak@gojcc.org

Purpose:
To help disadvantaged people obtain life's basic requirements: jobs, housing, clothing, access to benefits and food.

Programs:
Russian-English translation services, Russian cultural programs, Jewish cultural programs, community organizing, employment, housing, immigrant resettlement and adjustment, emergency problem-solving, case management, information and referral, nutrition services, meal program, connection to health services, landlord tenant resolution, financial assistance.

Website: www.gojcc.org

JEWISH AMERICAN

Friends of Refugees of Eastern Europe

2935 W. Devon Ave.
Chicago, IL 60659
(773) 274-5123

Contact:
Rabbi Shmuel Notik
exec. dir.
Email: lnotik@obshina.com

Purpose:
To promote needed social services and provide knowledge of Jewish heritage to Russian immigrant Jews.

Programs:
Judaic lessons, Hebrew Sunday School, bar/bat mitzvahs, circumcision, traditional Jewish weddings, counseling, citizenship, community center, community organizing, culture preservation, education, employment, family, language, heritage/history, immigrant resettlement and adjustment, recreation, referral, senior citizens, technical assistance, tutoring, women, youth, translating.

Website: www.obshina.com

Hadassah

4711 Golf Road, Suite 600
Skokie, IL 60076
(847) 675-6790

Contact:
Ronna Ash
ofc. mgr.
Email:
bigchapter.chicago@hadassah.org

Purpose:
To support two hospitals in Israel, schools and social benefits here and in Israel.

Programs:
Charitable support for health care, education and medical research.

Website: www.chicago.hadassah.org

Hebrew Immigrant Aid Society

216 West Jackson Blvd., Suite 700
Chicago, IL 60606
(312) 357-4666

Contact:
Susan Wexler
asst. dir.
Email: HIASchicago@jcfs.org

Purpose:
To help immigrants with things like Green Cards, and refugee & immigration services.

Programs:
Education, counseling & support, disabilities, residential and child welfare, community support (clinical conferences and training for health professionals, social work).

Website: http://www.jcfs.org/

JEWISH AMERICAN

The Hillels of Illinois

30 Wells St., Suite 216-600
Chicago, IL 60606
Phone: (312) 444-2868

Contact:
Rabbi Paul Z. Saiger
exec. dir.
Email: hillel@juf.org

Purpose:
To serve and represent Jewish university students and young adults.

Programs:
Arts, counseling, community organizing, culture preservation, education, heritage/history, mentoring, recreation, social/fraternal, tutoring, women, youth, social service. (Chapters at universities including UIC, Loyola, DePaul, Northwestern, U of I, U of C)

Website: www.thehillelsofillinois.org

Illinois Holocaust Museum & Education Center

9603 Woods Drive
Skokie, IL 60077
(847) 967-4800

Contact:
Richard S. Hirschhaut
exec. dir.
Email: info@ilhmec.org

Purpose:
To preserve the legacy of the Holocaust by honoring the memories of those who were lost and by teaching universal lessons that combat hatred, prejudice and indifference. The museum fulfills its mission through the exhibition, preservation and interpretation of its collections and through education programs and initiatives that foster the promotion of human rights and the elimination of genocide

Programs:
Museum featuring the Karkomi permanent exhibition, special temporary exhibitions, Miller Family Youth Exhibition, library and resource center, speakers' bureau, monthly community programs.

Website: http://www.ilholocaustmuseum.org/

Jewish Big Sisters

3150 N. Sheridan, #27B
Chicago, IL 60657
(312) 458-9003

Purpose:
To provide a mentoring program.

Programs:
Provide individual big sisters; recreational/cultural/religious events; social service counseling and referrals, camp scholarships, heritage/history, immigrant resettlement and adjustment.

JEWISH AMERICAN

Jewish Community Relations Council
(Jewish United Fund of Metro Chicago/ Jewish Federation)

30 South Wells St.
Chicago, IL 60606
(312) 357-4770

Contact:
Lisa C. Klein
assoc. dir.
Email: jcrc1@juf.org

Purpose:
As the community relations arm of the Jewish Federation/Jewish United Fund, to be the instrument through which the organized Jewish community collectively makes policy on the shared agenda of its constituent members.

Programs:
Information resource, education and advocacy, sponsors annual celebrations, coordinates programming, provides assistance, interfaith/intergroup relations.

Website: http://www.juf.org/jcrc

Jewish Council on Urban Affairs

610 S. Michigan Ave., Suite 500
Chicago, IL 60605
(312) 663-0960

Contact:
Katherine Randall
Email: jcuanews@jcua.org

Purpose:
To help people help themselves; to promote justice and build bridges of understanding among ethnic groups; to tackle bigotry in all forms.

Programs:
Providing echnical assistance to low-income communities, promoting just public policy, and educating and mobilizing the Jewish community on social and economic justice issues.

Website: www.jcua.org

Jewish Child & Family Services

216 W. Jackson Blvd., Suite 700
Chicago, IL 60606
(312) 357-4800

Contact:
Howard Sitron
CEO

Purpose:
To provide vital, individualized, results-driven services. to thousands of children, adults and families throughout the diverse Chicago community.

Programs:
Counseling, psychological testing, speech, occupational and developmental therapies, support for individuals with disabilities, special education, camps and recreation, and residential care for abused and neglected children. Has offices in Chicago (Downtown & West Rogers Park), Skokie, Northbrook, Arlington Heights, Flossmoor, Lombard.

Website: www.jcfs.org   **Blog:** www.jcfscommunities.org

JEWISH AMERICAN

JCC Chicago

30 S. Wells St., Suite 4000
Chicago, IL 60606
(312) 775-1801

Contact:
Martin Levine
gen. dir.
Email: info@gojcc.org

Purpose:
To ensure a strong, vibrant Jewish life and community for generations to come. Through a mix of formal and informal education, recreational and cultural activities, JCC Chicago provides quality experiences that enrich the lives of individuals, families and the community at large.

Programs:
Early childhood education, day and resident camp, children & family, after-school, recreational, adult, education, travel, family services, and volunteer opportunities. Locations: Skokie, Northbrook, Buffalo Grove, Lake Zurich, Glencoe, Hoffman Estates, Chicago, Rogers Park, Lakeview, Flossmoor, Hyde Park

Website: www.gojcc.org

Jewish Genealogical Society of Illinois

P.O. Box 515
Northbrook, IL 60065-0515
(312) 666-0100

Contact:
Mike Carson
pres.
Email: president@jgsi.org

Purpose:
To provide information on how and where to search for one's family "roots," as well as networking with other researchers.

Programs:
Advice on how to learn about one's personal heritage and history.

Website: www.jewishgen.org/jgsi/

Jewish Labor Committee

250 N. Michigan Ave., Suite 2100
Chicago, IL 60601
(312) 607-0260

Contact:
Eli Fishman
reg. dir.
Email: ChicagoJLC@yahoo.com

Purpose:
To be a liaison between the Jewish community and labor movement, as well as other ethnic labor organizations.

Programs:
Civil rights, heritage/history, politics, workers rights, labor unions.

Website: www.jewishlabor.org

JEWISH AMERICAN

Keshet

3210 Dundee Road
Northbrook, IL 60062
(847) 205-0274

Contact:
Abbie Weisberg
exec. dir.
Email: admin@kesshet.org

Purpose:
To serve needs of disabled Jewish children and their families.

Programs:
Day school, Sunday school, summer day camp and overnight camp for disabled Jewish children; support groups; parent education; referral. Other addresses: Bais Yaakov School, 6100 N. California; Ida Crown Jewish Academy, 2828 W. Pratt.

Website: www.keshet.org

New Israel Fund

Chicago Region
PO Box 1127
Highland Park, IL 60035
(847) 224-6360

Contact:
Jeryl Levin
reg. dir.
Email: Jeryl@nif.org

Purpose:
The New Israel Fund is the leading organization committed to equality and democracy for all Israelis. Widely credited with building Israel's progressive civil society from scratch, NIF has provided over $200 million to more than 800 cutting-edge organizations since our inception. Through our action arm SHATIL, we provide Israel's social change community with hands-on assistance. In addition, NIF/SHATIL builds coalitions, empowers activists, sponsors new programs, and takes the initiative in spearheading national advocacy campaigns.

Programs:
Civil and human rights; social and economic justice; religious pluralism and tolerance; Israeli Arabs and Bedouin citizens; women's rights; and environment.

Website: www.nif.org

Olin-Sang-Ruby Union Institute URJ

(Union for Reform Judaism)
555 Skokie Blvd., Suite 333
Northbrook, IL 60062
(847) 509-0990

Contact:
Gerard Kaye
exec. dir.
Email: osrui@urj.org

Purpose:
To provide a religious and educational camp and retreat center.

Programs:
Summer residential camp in Oconomowoc, WI; weekend programs for adults and families throughout the year.

Website: www.osrui.org

JEWISH AMERICAN

Spertus Institute of Jewish Studies

610 S. Michigan Ave.
Chicago, IL 60605
(312) 322-1700

Contact:
Dr. Hal Lewis
pres. & CEO
Email: SpertusPR@Spertus.edu

Purpose:
To be a center for Jewish learning and culture.

Programs:
Adult education; public programs; masters degrees in Jewish Studies, Jewish Professional Studies and Nonprofit Management; doctoral programs in Jewish Studies; nonprofit certificate workshops.

Website: www.spertus.edu/

Women's American ORT

3701 Commercial Ave., Suite 13
Northbrook, IL 60062
(847) 291-0475

Contact:
Stephanie Pritzker
dir. of dev.
Email: Chicago@ortamerica.org

Purpose:
Jewish organization committed to strengthening communities throughout the world by educating people against all odds and obstacles.

Programs:
Resale shops, tribute cards, events, interest groups.

Website: www.ortamerica.org/chicago

Zarem/Golde ORT Technical Institute

5440 W. Fargo Ave.
Skokie, IL 60077
(847) 324-5588

Contact:
Marina Chudnovsky
dir.
Email: info@zg-ort.edu

Purpose:
To train students in ESL, technical programs and medical programs and to provide career services and job placement.

Programs:
Associate degrees in accounting, computerized accounting, IT support and networking; visual graphics and web design, medical assistant, medical office administration, pharmacy technician, ESL and TOEFL preparation.

Website: www.zg-ort.edu/

KOREAN AMERICAN

Hanul Family Alliance
(formerly Korean American Senior Center)

5008 N. Kedzie Avenue
Chicago, IL 60625
Phone: (773) 478-8851

Contact:
Paul Yun
exec. dir.
Email: hanul@hanulusa.org

Purpose:
To empower individuals and families in need to enhance the quality of life.

Programs:
ESL, home care, crime-victim assistance, information, referral, case management, arts & culture, citizenship, health seminars, financial literacy, congregate meals, energy assistance.

Website: www.hanulusa.org

Korean-American Association of Chicago

5941 N. Lincoln Ave.
Chicago, IL 60659
(773) 878-1900

Contact:
John J. Kim
exec. dir.
Email: kaac29@koreachicago.org

Purpose:
To provide human services for immigrants adjusting to a new environment.

Programs:
Naturalization assistance, counseling, community employment program.

Website: www.koreachicago.org

Korean American Chamber of Commerce

5601 N. Spaulding
Chicago, IL 60659
(773) 583-1700

Contact:
Brandon Yu
exec. dir.
Email: ckacc@ckacc.org

Purpose:
To provide assistance to small businesses owned by Korean Americans.

Programs:
Business and professional support, counseling, economic development, financial aid, referral, technical assistance.

Website: www.ckacc.org

KOREAN AMERICAN

Korean American Coalition of Chicago (KACC)

5903 N. Campbell Ave., Unit 2
Chicago, IL 60659

Contact:
Eugene Chang
pres. at echang@kac-chicago.org or
Karen Hwang,
V.P. at khwang@kac-chicago.org
Email: kacchicago@gmail.com

Purpose:
To promote the civic participation of Korean Americans through advocacy, community service, leadership development, and cultural education. Our goal is to create a strong, vibrant community that embraces the best of our Korean heritage and the potential of our future in America.

Programs:
Generation KAC ("GenKAC" - annual networking gala); KACC Get Connected! (networking socials); KACC Speaker Series (local and national KA notable figures); KA Community Calendar (community calendar for KA organizations); KACC Mentorship Pipeline (young professionals career guidance); KACC Partners (Collaboration with other organizations); Leadership Development; KACC Flavor of Chicago (user-based reviews of KA businesses).

Website: www.kac-chicago.org

Korean American Community Services

4300 N. California
Chicago, IL 60618
(773) 583-5501

Contact:
InChul Choi
exec. dir.
Email: inchul@kacschicago.org

Purpose:
To empower all members of the community by providing educational, legal, health, and social services so that all may fulfill their needs and live dignified and meaningful lives.

Programs:
Individual and group counseling; crisis intervention; domestic violence support services; emergency cash and food assistance; toddler, preschool and after school programs; school social work; immigration and naturalization assistance; workforce development and job placement assistance; ESL and civics classes; arts and culture classes; IT classes/community computer lab; senior services and public benefits assistance; health education and outreach; free and low-cost health screening services; and bi-annual health fairs.

Website: www.kacschicago.org

KOREAN AMERICAN

Korean American Women in Need

P.O. Box 59133
Chicago, IL 60659
(773) 583-1392

Contact:
Youngju Ji
exec. dir.
Email: info@kanwin.org

Purpose:
To serve Asian American immigrant victims of domestic violence and sexual assault.

Programs:
24-hour crisis hotline (773) 583-0880; crisis intervention; case management; legal and social advocacy; children's program; transitional housing program; counseling and support groups; long-term empowerment services; referral; community education.

Website: www.kanwin.org

Korean American Women's Association of Chicago

9930 Capitol Drive, Suite 909
Wheeling, IL 60090
(773) 742-1456

Contact:
Kyu Young Park
pres.
Email: kawaoc@gmail.com

Purpose:
To bring Korean American women to a new maturity by sharing experiences and providing mutual support.

Programs:
Korean Women's Talk Line, Women's Corner, Korean Women's Choir, seminars and workshops and community participation.

Website: http://kawac.org

Korean Cultural Center of Chicago

9930 Capitol Dr.
Wheeling, IL 60090
(847) 947-4460
Email: programdirector@kccoc.org

Purpose:
To promote and organize Korean cultural, educational, art, and social activities for the public.

Programs:
Museum, art gallery, library, dance studio, Korean language, Korean history, variety of other classes.

Website: www.kccoc.org

KOREAN AMERICAN

Korean YMCA of Chicago

5820 N. Lincoln Ave.
Chicago, IL 60659
(773) 275-0101

Contact:
John Kim

Purpose:
To help new Korean immigrants adjust in the American community.

Programs:
ESL, foreign language classes (Chinese, Japanese, Spanish, etc.), swimming, winter sports, drug prevention, matchmaking counseling, guest house for tourists and people with family problems, financial and legal instruction, vocational training, cultural classes.

Korean YWCA

4753 North Broadway
Chicago, Illinois 60640
(773) 596.5490

Contact:
Gina Lee

Purpose:
To empower Korean American women in the Chicago metro area.

Programs:
Bilingual services, Korean Domestic Violence Program.

LAO AMERICAN

Lao American Community Services

4750 N. Sheridan Road, Suite 369
Chicago, IL, 60640
(773) 271-0004

Contact:
Thavone Nyatso
exec. dir.
Email: info@lacschicago.org

Purpose:
To assist refugees and immigrants from Laos residing in Illinois, especially those in metropolitan Chicago, to become self-sufficient, productive participants in American society while preserving and enhancing their cultural heritage, identity, and their sense of belonging to a community.

Programs:
Case management, citizenship & EL/civics classes, health care outreach & education, assistance in public benefits application, referrals and assistance in immigration applications.

Website: www.lacschicago.org

LATVIAN AMERICAN

Chicago Latvian Assn.
4146 N. Elston Ave.
Chicago, IL 60618
(773) 588-2085

Contact:
Ray Kalnajs

Purpose:
To offer a variety of social and cultural services for the Latvian community.

Programs:
Museum, folk art museum, concerts, dance classes other arts and cultural activities, community center, support groups, counseling.

LEBANESE AMERICAN

Midwest Federation of Syrian & Lebanese Clubs
P.O. Box 6835
Villa Park, IL 60181-6835
Email: jhaddad630@aol.com

Contact:
Jackie Haddad
chr.

Purpose:
To promote and preserve the ethnic heritage of its members, to advance the scholarship of its youth, and to support humanitarian causes.

Programs:
Scholarships for students, humanitarian efforts, charity events, ethnic fairs, political rights advocacy .

Website: www.midwestfederation.net

Lebanese Club of Chicago
P.O. Box 81584
Chicago, IL 60681-0584
(847) 549-9417

Contact:
Hoda Movagh
pres.
Email: CLC@chicagolebaneseclub.org

Purpose:
To preserve, enrich and promote the Lebanese culture and to serve the Lebanese Community in and outside of Chicago through cultural, educational, humanitarian and social activities.

Programs:
Family activities, sports events, charity events, health and financial advocacy.

Website: www.leb.net/clc

LIBERIAN AMERICAN

Liberian Emergency Relief Fund

2214 E. 75th St.
Chicago, IL 60649
(773) 643-8635

Contact:
Alexander P. Gbayee
exec. dir.
Email: LibCon20032@yahoo.com

Purpose:
To give charitable assistance to displaced Liberians and Liberian refugees.

Programs:
Housing, clothing, food, medicine, transportation, public education, translating.

Organization of Liberian Communities in Illinois

P.O. Box 377644
Chicago, IL 60637-7644
(708) 250-4223

Contact:
Richard Tamba
pres. (773) 474-3686
Email: president@olci.org

Purpose:
To promote and enhance public awareness of the culture and history of Liberia; to provide assistance to members in matters of immigration, employment, housing.

Programs:
Immigration, employment, community organizing, culture preservation, social/fraternal.

Website: www.olci.org

LITHUANIAN AMERICAN

Balzekas Museum of Lithuanian Culture

6500 S. Pulaski Road
Chicago, IL 60629-5136
(773) 582-6500

Contact:
Stanley Balzekas, Jr.
pres.
Email: info@balzekasmuseum.org

Purpose:
To preserve posterity and the wealth of material pertaining to Lithuania and Lithuanians, and to serve as a resource and research center for students and scholars.

Programs:
Lectures, workshops, exhibits, audio-visual programs, seminars in genealogy, resource center, archives, translating.

Website: www.balzekasmuseum.org

LITHUANIAN AMERICAN

Lithuanian-American Community Human Services Council

2711-15 W. 71st Street
Chicago, IL 60629
(773) 476-2655

Contact:
Joe Polikaitis
exec. dir.
Email: LHServices@sbcglobal.net

Purpose:
To help Lithuanians with various social needs.

Programs:
Lithuanian Children's Hope, Lithuanian orphan care, aid to newcomers to the USA, senior citizens, letter translation.

Lithuanian Foundation, Inc.

14911 127th St.
Lemont, IL 60439
(630) 257-1616

Contact:
Marius Kasniunas
exec. dir.
Email: admin@lithfund.org

Purpose:
To support the survival of Lithuanian cultural and educational endeavors in multi-ethnic and multi-cultural USA.

Programs:
Culture preservation, education, heritage/history, youth scholarships.

Website: www.lithuanianfoundation.org

Lithuanian Mercy Lift

P.O. Box 88
Palos Heights, IL 60463
(708) 636-6140

Contact:
Ausrine Karaitis
pres.
Email: lithuanianmercylift@yahoo.com

Purpose:
To provide humanitarian medical aid to Lithuania.

Programs:
Sending or procuring medical equipment and supplies to Lithuania's hospitals, clinics, orphanages and senior homes, and supporting autism, diabetes, suicide prevention, oral hygiene and mammogram programs.

Website: www.lithuanianmercylift.org

LITHUANIAN AMERICAN

Lithuanian Research & Studies Center

5600 S. Claremont Ave.
Chicago, IL 60636-1039
Phone: (773) 434-4545

Contact:
Dr. Augustinas Jdzelis
pres.
Email: info@lithuanianresearch.org

Purpose:
To preserve documentation and artifacts of Lithuanian culture and activities of Lithuanian Americans and to meet needs of researchers interested in these subjects.

Programs:
Arts, culture preservation, education, foreign aid (books), heritage/history, language, research, Lithuanian Historical Society, Lithuanian Institute of Education, Lithuanian Museum of Medicine, translation.

Website: www.lithuanianresearch.org

Lithuanian World Center

14911 127th St.
Lemont, IL 60439
(630) 257-8787

Contact:
Jolanta Kurpis
Email: admin@lcenter.org

Purpose:
To serve as an exchange center between Lithuania and America's Lithuanian community, and to keep the culture and customs alive

Programs:
Montessori school, Saturday school, Catholic mission, art museum, halls for cultural and social events, athletic facilities, library for archives and exhibits, rehearsal rooms, office space for Lithuanian organizations.

Website: www.lcenter.org

Lithuanian Youth Center

5620 S. Claremont Ave.
Chicago, IL 60629
(773) 778-7500

Contact:
Zigmas Mikuzis
pres.

Purpose:
To provide a facility for Lithuanian American activity.

Programs:
Saturday School, cultural and social gatherings, art gallery, museum, archives.

MUSLIM AMERICAN

Council on American-Islamic Relations (CAIR Chicago)

28 E. Jackson Blvd, Suite 1700
Chicago, IL 60604
(312) 212-1520

Contact:
Mazen Kudaimi, MD
pres.
Email: info@cairchicago.org

Purpose:
To promote an accurate image of Islam and Muslims in America.

Programs:
Media relations, conferences and seminars, publications and action alerts to advocate for American Muslim rights and relations.

Website: http://www.cairchicago.org/

Chicago Islamic Cultural Ctr.

3357 W. 63 St.
Chicago, IL 60629
(773) 436-8083

Purpose:
To offer a space for Muslims to pray and meet with other Muslims in the Chicago area.

Programs:
Daily and Friday prayers, special Ramadan programs.

Inner-City Muslim Action Network

2744 West 63rd St.
Chicago, IL 60629
(773) 434-4626

Contact:
Rami Nashashibi
exec. dir.
Email: info@imancentral.org

Purpose:
To foster a space for Muslims in urban America by inspiring the larger community towards civic engagement and to work for social justice and human dignity across religions, ethnicities, and nationalities.

Programs:
Arts, musical and cultural events, political and social advocacy, youth development and engagement, internships.

Website: www.imancentral.org

Islamic Cultural Center of Greater Chicago

1810 N. Pfingsten Road
Northbrook, IL 60062
(847) 272-0319

Purpose:
To bring together Muslims in the Northbrook area.

Programs:
Friday prayers, Saturday/Sunday Islamic school for children.

MUSLIM AMERICAN

The Council of Islamic Organizations of Greater Chicago (CIOGC)

231 S. State St., Suite 300
Chicago IL 60604
(800) 678-0753

Contact:
Dr. Zaher Sahloul
chair

Purpose:
To be the unifying federation of Islamic organizations of Greater Chicago, the leading advocate of Muslim community interests and a catalyst for enriching American Society.

Programs:
Networking, interfaith events, political and social rights advocacy, charity, educational and recreational events.

Muslim Community Center

4380 N. Elston Ave.
Chicago, IL 60641
(773) 725-9047

Contact:
Mohammad Aleemuddin
pres.

Purpose:
To serve the metropolitan Chicago area and the Muslim community within it. Established in 1969.

Programs:
Five daily prayers, Friday prayers, education through full- and part-time schools, adult education programs, health programs, marriage ceremonies, special programs for women and youth, special Ramadan programs, charity events/programs, funeral arrangements and facilities, outreach and interfaith programs.

Website: http://www.mccchicago.org/

Muslim Education Center

8601 N. Menard Ave.
Morton Grove, IL 60053
(847) 470-8801

Contact:
Habeeb Quadri
principal
Email: contact@mccfts.org

Purpose:
A state-accredited elementary school that aims to educate students in the northern suburbs by including both secular and Islamic studies courses.

Programs:
Early childhood, middle-school programs, Qur'an memorization program, extracurricular activities, athletics, Saturday/Sunday Islamic schools, community gatherings, Friday prayers.

Website: http://mccfts.org/

NATIVE AMERICAN

American Indian Health Service of Chicago, Inc.

4081 N. Broadway
Chicago, IL 60613
(773) 883-9100

Contact:
Dr. Ashley Nix-Allen
medical dir.
Email: ahealthser@aol.com

Purpose:
To provide sensitive and holistic health care for Native Americans.

Programs:
General health care, prevention and intervention, dentistry, substance abuse, mental health, HIV/AIDS prevention, Four Directions after-school study program

Website: www.aihschicago.org

American Indian Center

1630 W. Wilson Ave.
Chicago, IL 60640
(773) 275-5871

Contact:
Joe Podlasek
exec. *dir.*
Email: aic50@aic-chicago.org

Purpose:
Providing cultural education and meeting the needs of the Native community via education, wellness and arts.

Programs:
Arts, tutoring and mentoring children, community center, culture preservation, family, heritage/history, senior citizens, veterans, youth.

Website: www.aic-chicago.org

Kateri Center of Chicago
(formerly Anawim Center)

3938 N. Leavitt
Chicago, IL 60618
(773) 509-2344

Contact:
Georgina Roy
dir.
Email: groy@archchicago.org

Purpose:
Kateri Center of Chicago is a ministry of the Archdiocese of Chicago serving a community of American Indian Catholics through faith formation and Native traditional prayer.

Programs:
Advocacy for indigenous rights, artists cooperative, religious ceremonies (Christian and Traditional Native American), information and referral, youth.

Website: www.katericenterchicago.org

NATIVE AMERICAN

Mitchell Museum of the American Indian

3001 Central Park
Evanston, IL 60201
(847) 475-1030

Contact:
Kathleen McDonald
exec. dir.

Purpose:
To maintain a collection representing native peoples of the USA and Canada.

Programs:
Reference library includes books, periodicals, videos, audio tapes; gift shop sells Native American pottery, jewelry, fetishes, books; permanent exhibits on hunting and harvesting by peoples of western Great Lakes, buffalo hunters of northern plains, Pueblo farmers and pastoral Navajo.

Website: www.mitchellmuseum.org

St. Augustine Center for American Indians, Inc.

4512 N. Sheridan Road
Chicago, IL 60640
(773) 784-1050

Contact:
Fr. Peter J. Powell

Purpose:
To serve the Native American people in metro Chicago

Programs:
Religious and social services, Indian Child Welfare, Program Excel (education), alcohol/substance abuse prevention and rehabilitation.

NIGERIAN AMERICAN

Nigerian Community of Chicagoland

28 East Jackson Blvd. Suite 600
P.O. Box 20570
Chicago, IL 60620
(773) 651-9098

Contact:
David Olupitan
chair.
Email: info@chicago-nigerians.org

Purpose:
To unite Nigerian organizations and individuals in the Chicago area to advance the interests of Nigeria and Nigerians.

Programs:
Professional development, business development, educational development, cultural awareness, involvement in local civic activities.

Website: www.Chicago-nigerians.org

NORWEGIAN AMERICAN

Norwegian American Chamber of Commerce, Midwest-Chicago Chapter

Consul General of Norway
125 S. Wacker Dr., Suite 1825
Chicago, IL 60606
(312) 377-5050, (847) 530-4101

Contact:
Mette Bowen
pres.
Email: mette.m.bowen@comcast.net

Purpose:
To promote trade and goodwill and foster business, financial and professional interests between Norway and the United States; to advance common purposes of members.

Programs:
Business or professional support through monthly lunch or dinner meetings, field trips to member companies, networking, membership directory, social events.

Website: www.naccchicago.org

Norwegian National League of Chicago

715 Laurel Ave.
Des Plaines, IL, 60016
(847) 297-1656

Contact:
Lynn Sove Maxson
dir.
Email: sovmax@wowway.com

Purpose:
To work for perpetuation and strengthening of interest in Norwegian traditions and culture; to support Norwegian and Norwegian-American organizations; to arrange holiday festivals.

Programs:
Norway Constitution Day (May 17), Lief Erickson Fest (Oct. 9) and Christmas Around the World; rosemaling (traditional painting), folk dancing, translating.

Website: www.nnleague.org

PAKISTANI AMERICAN

Association of Physicians of Pakistani Descent of North America (APPNA)

6414 South Cass Ave.
Westmont, IL 60559
(630) 968-8585

Contact:
Zubair M. Syed, *MD*
Email: info@appna.org

Purpose:
To promote health care, research, education, humanitarian activities through the united effort of Pakistani and Pakistani-American physicians.

Programs:
Advocacy, charitable projects, health-care facilities nationwide, annual convention.

Website: http://www.appna.org

PAKISTANI AMERICAN

Organization of Pakistani Entrepreneurs and Professionals

Email: info@open-chicago.org

Contact:
Ruma Samdani
sec.

Purpose:
To raise the profile of Chicago-area Pakistani entrepreneurial and professional community and to foster collaboration and provide guidance on entrepreneurship in association with regional academic centers.

Programs:
Speaker events, mentoring programs, networking events.

Website: http://www.open-chicago.org/

Pakistan Federation of America, Chicago

P.O. Box 60101
Chicago, IL 60660
(773) 556-9993

Contact:
Hameedullah Khan
chair
Email: pfachicago@mail.com

Purpose:
To be the leading Pakistani-American community organization for multipurpose uses.

Programs:
Arts and cultural activities, business and professional support, citizenship and immigration seminar, employment workshop, recreation, social, translating on request.

Pakistani American Bar Association

Contact:
Saadia Siddique
pres.
(312) 854-8060
(president's work number)
Email: ssiddique@krilaw.com

Purpose:
To promote the professional development and career advancement of Pakistani American legal professionals.

Programs:
Networking opportunities, continuing legal education, and opportunities to participate in pro bono clinics.

Website: www.pabalaw.org

YOUR DIL Chicago

Email: chicago@yourdil.org

Contact:
Mazhar Masud
pres.

Purpose:
A non-profit organization working to advance literacy in remote and neglected areas of Pakistan.

Programs:
Fundraising events, dinners, speaker events.

Website: http://www.yourdil.org/

PALESTINIAN AMERICAN

Ramallah Club of Chicago

2700 N. Central Ave.
Chicago, IL 60639
(773) 237-2727, (773) 934-5819

Contact:
Kenny Agal
mgr.

Purpose:
To help a community that traces its origins to the village of Ramallah to maintain its ties, heritage and culture.

Programs:
Arabic school, yearly convention with other branches across U.S., family parties, youth activities.

POLISH AMERICAN

Advocates Society

P.O. Box 641883
Chicago, IL, 60664-1833
(773) 267-6100

Contact:
Robert Groszek
pres.
Email: advocatessociety@gmail.com

Purpose:
To provide professional, social and ethnic activities that relate to the practice of law and development of legal skills and knowledge.

Programs:
Legal clinic, scholarships, formal dinner dance, judges reception and annual installation dinner.

Website: www.advocatesociety.com

Copernicus Foundation

5216 W. Lawrence Ave.
Chicago, IL 60630
(773) 777-8898

Contact:
Patrizia Fuchs
event coord.
Email: Copernicus@ameritech.net

Purpose:
To promote theater and cultural shows and performances for various cultural groups in Chicago area, including Polish events.

Programs:
Taste of Polonia, Copernican Awards, culture preservation, community center, education, ESL, cultural shows, farmers market.

Website: www.copernicusfdn.org

POLISH AMERICAN

Gift from the Heart Foundation

3860 N. 25th Avenue
Schiller Park, IL 60176
(847) 671-2711

Contact:
Izabel Rybak
exec. dir.
Email: info@giftheart.org

Purpose:
To help disabled children.

Programs:
Buy rehab equipment; provide food, lodging, transport and interpreters for children from abroad; learn about available medical care for disabled children; provide respite care for needy families with disabled members; counseling, education, translating.

Website: www.darserca.org

Kosciuszko Foundation

325 S. Chester
Park Ridge, IL 60068
(847) 698-0250

Contact:
Prof. Lidia Filus
Email: L-Filus@nelu.edu

Purpose:
Cultural/educational exchange and scholarships.

Programs:
Polish-language summer scholarships, Polish American cultural events, annual Chopin piano competition, recital.

Website: www.thekf.org

Lira Company

6525 N. Sheridan Rd., Suite 905
Chicago, IL 60626
(773) 508-7040

Contact:
Lucyna Migala
gen. mgr., art. dir.

Purpose:
To help acquaint Polish Americans with the richness of their thousand-year-old heritage of music and dance, and help other Americans learn about and appreciate Polish culture and traditions.

Programs:
Performances by the Lira Company, consisting of the Lira Singers, Chamber Chorus, Chamber Orchestra, Children's Chorus and Dancers; artist in residence at Loyola; outreach concerts to and with several major ethnic communities in Chicago; recordings; translating, Christmas Gala program.

POLISH AMERICAN

PNA Polish Information Center-Amicus Poloniae Free Legal Clinic

5711 N. Milwaukee Ave.
Chicago, IL 60646
(773) 763-8520

Contact:
Mark Dobrzycki
exec. dir. of Information Center
Email: pnainfocenter@pna-znp.org

Purpose:
Information Center: to provide information about the Polish community in Chicago. U.S. Legal Clinic: to provide legal services to Polish-speaking community of Chicago and others.

Programs:
Information and resources; general legal advice, legal representation, referrals to attorneys, client intake on the third Saturday of the month.

Polish American Association

3834 N. Cicero Ave.
Chicago, IL 60641
(773) 282-8206

Contact:
Karen Popowski
exec. dir.
Email: paa@polish.org

Purpose:
To be a comprehensive Polish bilingual and bicultural social-service agency.

Programs:
Counseling, citizenship, education, employment, food pantry, health screenings, homeless outreach, immigrant adjustment, senior citizen, shelter for homeless men, substance-abuse treatment, vocational training, women, youth, advocacy.
Other office: 6276 W. Archer Ave., (773) 767-7773

Website: http://www.polish.org

Polish American Congress

5711 N. Milwaukee Ave.
Chicago, IL 60646-6294
(773) 763-9944

Contact:
Timothy Kurza
Email: pacchgo@pac1944.com

Purpose:
To serve as an umbrella organization of more than 3,000 organizations and clubs and to further knowledge of Polish history, language and culture as well as stimulate Polish American involvement and accomplishments.

Programs:
Civic, education, culture preservation, fraternal, heritage/history, veteran, religious, professional; humanitarian aid for Poland through the PAC Charitable Foundation.

Website: www.pac1944.org

POLISH AMERICAN

Polish American Congress, Illinois Division

5844 N. Milwaukee Ave.
Chicago, IL 60646
(773) 631-3300

Contact:
Mary Anselmo
pres.
Email: contact@pac-il.org

Purpose:
To stimulate and unify people of Polish descent, and to help people in Poland.

Programs:
English language classes, immigration and naturalization assistance, translation of legal documents such as births, marriages, deaths.

Website: www.pac-il.org

Polish Arts Club of Chicago

P.O. Box 30169
Chicago, IL 60630
(773) 278-7155

Contact:
Jessica Jagielnik
pres.

Purpose:
Appreciation of the arts.

Programs:
Art exhibitions, literary competition, art & book fair, recitals, scholarships based on artistic merit, club for people who appreciate all forms of art.

Polish Genealogical Society of America

984 N. Milwaukee Ave.
Chicago, IL 60622

Contact:
Brian Doornbos
exec. dir.
Email: PGSAmerica@pgsa.org

Purpose:
Help Poles trace genealogy.

Programs:
Conferences, workshops, genealogical trips for personal research, publications and books.

Website: www.pgsa.org

Polish Museum of America

984 N. Milwaukee Ave.
Chicago, IL 60642-4101
(773) 384-3352

Contact:
Jan Lorys
dir.
Email:
pma@polishmuseumofamerica.org

Purpose:
To uphold and promote Polish and Polish American history and culture through programs, lectures and performances.

Programs:
Arts; culture preservation; education; research; archives with 60,000 volumes, 250 periodicals, Polish and American music collection; translating (limited).

Website: www.polishmuseumofamerica.org

POLISH AMERICAN

Polish National Alliance

6100 N. Cicero Ave.
Chicago, IL 60646
(773) 286-0500

Contact:
Frank Spula
pres.
Email: pna@pna-znp.org,
frank.spula@pna-znp.org

Purpose:
To provide insurance protection and serve the ethnic community.

Programs:
Scholarships, education, sports, youth, seniors, cultural (ethnic press, radio, cultural events).

Website: www.pna-znp.org

Polish Roman Catholic Union of America

984 N. Milwaukee Ave.
Chicago, IL 60622
(773) 782-2600

Contact:
James J. Robaczewski
sec.-treas.
Email: info@prcua.org

Purpose:
To strengthen and preserve spiritual values, patriotic zeal, ethnic culture and heritage; and to foster cultural relations between the USA and Poland.

Programs:
Life insurance, fraternal, sports teams, language classes, crafts, youth festivals, folk dancing, singing, scholarships, museum patron, archives, art exhibits, awards to outstanding Polish Americans.

Polish Scouting Organization of Illinois

6434 W. Belmont Ave.
Chicago, IL 60634
(773) 481-2718

Contact:
Barbara Chalko
exec. dir.
Email: zhpchicago@gmail.com

Purpose:
To provide educational programs, based on ideals of world scouting, that develop character, strength of mind, body and soul, patriotism and good citizenship; to preserve Polish culture and heritage.

Programs:
Scout, Brownie, Cub and Daisy troops.

Website: www.zhpchicago.com

Polish Women's Alliance of America

6643 N. Northwest Highway, 2nd Floor
Chicago, IL 60031
(847) 384-1200

Contact:
Virginia Sikora
pres.
Email: president@pwaa.org

Purpose:
To provide fraternal benefit life insurance and promote the Polish culture.

Programs:
Dance classes, language, youth, assisting immigrants with insurance plans, scholarships, social events.

Website: www.pwaa.org

POLISH AMERICAN

Polish Women's Civic Club, Inc

1015 Cypress Drive
Arlington Heights, IL 60005
(847) 394-2520

Contact:
Camille Kopielski
past pres.

Purpose:
To provide scholarships to qualified Polish American college students, philanthropy, fellowships.

Programs:
Contributions to hospitals, museums, institutions for needy and aged; scholarships, business luncheon, Palm Sunday luncheon, fundraisers.

PUERTO RICAN

Institute of Puerto Rican Arts & Culture

3015 Division St.
Chicago, IL 60622
(773) 486-8345

Contact:
Jose Lopez
exec. dir.
Email: info@iprac.com

Purpose:
To create and sustain a national museum to showcase Puerto Rican arts and historic exhibitions year-round, and to provide high-quality cultural programming.

Programs:
Arts education and outreach, a home for a permanent collection of Puerto Rican art, Barrio Arts Festival and Puerto Rican Film Series.

Website: www.iprac.org

Puerto Rican Cultural Center

2739 W. Division St.
Chicago, IL 60622
(773) 342-8023

Contact:
Zenida Lopez
Email: info@prcc-chgo.org

Purpose:
Multi-purpose agency.

Programs:
Arts, community organizing, culture preservation, day care, economic development, education, health care, HIV-testing, heritage/history, research, youth, high school.

Website: www.prcc-chgo.org

ROMANIAN AMERICAN

Illinois Romanian American Community

3938 W. Irving Park Road
Chicago, IL 60618
(773) 509-0010

Contact:
Octavian Cojan
pres.

Purpose:
To help Romanian-American community keep in touch with each other, local institutions and relatives in Romania. To promote cultural traditions.

Programs:
Events, Romanian festivals and celebrations.

Romanian-American Network

Romanian Heritage Center
7777 N. Caldwell Ave., Suite 103
Niles, IL 60714-3320
(847) 663-9690 or (708)243-2727 (cell)

Contact:
Steven V. Bonica
pres.
Email: romanianfest@gmail.com

Purpose:
Providing opportunities and custom tailored solutions for networking and communication outreaching to the Romanian-American community at large, or to certain trades and/or professional fields.

Programs:
Social-cultural & educational, networking, international business & trade, special events and community festivals, publishing & advertising, and more. Brand products / venues: Romanian Tribune Newspaper, Romanian-American Yellow Pages, Romanian Heritage Festival, Romanian-American Web Network

Website: www.ro-am.net

SCANDINAVIAN AMERICAN

Center for Scandinavian Studies

North Park University
3225 W. Foster Ave.
Chicago, IL 60625
(773) 244-5615

Contact:
Charles Peterson
dir.
Email: cpeterson@northpark.edu

Purpose:
To provide educational exchanges with Scandinavia and cultural programming with the countries of Scandinavia: Denmark, Finland, Iceland, Norway, and Sweden.

Programs:
Student and faculty exchanges with Scandinavian universities, guest lectures, exhibits and performances, archives, reference and translation services.

Website: www.northpark.edu/centers/center-for-scandinavian-studies

(See also Finnish, Norwegian, Swedish)

SCOTTISH AMERICAN

Chicago Scots: The Scottish Home of the Illinois Saint Andrew Society

2800 Des Plaines Ave.
North Riverside, IL 60546
(708) 447-5092
Email: info@chicagoscots.org

Purpose:
To nourish Scottish identity through service, fellowship and celebration of Scottish culture.

Programs:
Elder care: The Scottish Home (assisted living & nursing care). scholarships for study in Scotland, outreach to local schools, Scottish Festival & Highland Games, banquets, golf outings, conferences, Scottish American Museum, Scottish American Hall of Fame, Scottish History Club, Scottish Genealogy Society, Scottish Business Forum, Scottish Law Society.

Website: www.chicagoscots.org

SLOVAK AMERICAN

Slovak USA

1640 N. North Park Ave
Chicago, IL 60614
(312) 404-8104

Contact:
Igor Mikolaska
pres.
Email: info@slovakchicago.org

Purpose:
To promote cultural heritage of Slovaks in Chicago area and connect people of Slovak descent in local communities and throughout the United States.

Programs:
Cultural, educational, research, festival.

Website: http://www.slovakchicago.org/

SOMALI AMERICAN

Somaliland Community of Metro Chicago

6328 N. Bell #3
Chicago, IL 60659
(312) 576-1074

Contact:
Hussein Affey
Email: husseinaffey@gmail.com

Purpose:
To help the Somali Community in the Chicago area through social services.

Programs:
Health care issues, English language training, referrals to service providers.

SUDANESE AMERICAN

Sudanese Community Center

131 W. Jefferson St.
Naperville, IL 60540
(312) 576-8822

Contact:
Sean Tenner
bd. member
Email:
Sean@sudanesecommunitycenter.org

Purpose:
To link Illinois residents of Sudanese descent to services; to be a hub for the Chicago area's humanitarian efforts geared toward ending the suffering in Sudan.

Programs:
Referrals for day care, adult education, job training, health care, transportation, financial literacy course and ESL; hosts community meetings and educational forums.

Website: www.sudanesecommunitycenter.org

SWEDISH AMERICAN

Central Swedish Committee of Chicago,

c/o B. Pearson
4646 Larch
Glenview, IL 60025
(708) 747-4717

Contact:
Linda Tylk
Email: nilsson@utlx.com

Purpose:
Representation and continuity in the Swedish American community.

Programs:
Civic/fraternal, cultural/arts, children's groups with traditional ethnic programs, coordination with mayor's and governor's office, Swedish holiday celebrations, calendar of events, coordination with Swedish consulate

Website: www.centralswedishcommittee.com

SWEDISH AMERICAN

Swedish-American Chamber of Commerce

150 N. Michigan Ave., Suite 2800
Chicago, IL 60601
(312) 863-8592

Contact:
Gunn Johnsson
exec. dir
Email: sacc@sacc-chicago.org

Purpose:
To promote trade and commerce between Sweden and Chicago and the Midwest.

Programs:
Business matchmaking & trade missions, networking, cultural events such as Annual Golf Outing, Crayfish Event and Lucia Luncheon.

Website: www.sacc-chicago.org

Swedish-American Historical Society

3225 W. Foster Ave., Box 48
Chicago, IL 60625
(773) 244-5295, 244-5592

Contact:
Karin Andersson
ofc. mgr.
Email: info@swedishamericanhist.org

Purpose:
Historical, publications.

Programs:
Quarterly scholarly journal, programs, lectures, conferences, culture preservation, education, heritage/history, research.

Website: www.swedishamericanhist.org

Swedish American Museum

5211 N. Clark St.
Chicago, IL 60640
(773) 728-8111

Contact:
Karin Moen Abercrombie
exec. dir.
Email: museum@samac.org

Purpose:
To be a focal point for Swedish and Swedish American activities and the preservation of Swedish heritage.

Programs:
Permanent exhibit on Swedish immigration to Chicago, temporary exhibits on contemporary Swedish culture, classes, concerts, lectures, celebration of holidays.

Website: www.swedishamericanmuseum.org

Swedish Cultural Society in America

1123 S. Courtland
Park Ridge, IL 60068
(847) 825-8408

Contact:
Per-Hugo Kristensson
pres.

Purpose:
To promote Swedish heritage in America.

Programs:
Arts, concerts, lectures, business and professional support, education, family, heritage/history, immigrant resettlement, language, senior citizen, social/fraternal, translating.

TIBETAN AMERICAN

Tibetan Alliance of Chicago

2422 Dempster St.
Evanston, IL 60202
(847) 733-1111

Contact:
Norbu Samphell
pres.
Email: norsamT@aol.com

Purpose:
To empower the community and foster further development.

Programs:
Employment, English instruction, health care, housing, sponsorship, visa processing, promotion of awareness of Tibetan struggle, cultural performances, events, translating.

Website: www.tibetan-alliance.org

TIBETcenter

6073 N. Paulina
Chicago, IL 60660
(773) 743-7772

Contact:
Tashi Phuri
exec. dir.
Email: tibetcenter@aol.com

Purpose:
To preserve and promote the cultural heritage of Tibet and provide a venue for Tibetan and Buddhist studies.

Programs:
Arts, culture, preservation, translating.

Website: http://www.buddhapia.com/tibet/tibetcen, www.tibetcenterchicago.org

UKRAINIAN AMERICAN

Ukrainian Congress Committee of America, Illinois Division

2247 W. Chicago Ave.
Chicago, IL 60622
(847) 989-6634

Contact:
Dr. Alex Striltschuk
pres.
Email: uccaillinois@yahoo.com

Purpose:
Umbrella organization for Ukrainian civic, religious, cultural, social and youth organizations in Illinois. Representing the Ukrainian America community in Chicago and the state of Illinois since 1974.

Programs:
Coordination, Ukrainian Festival sponsor, advocacy, forums, ESL classes, assistance for new immigrants.

Website: www.uccaillinois.org

UKRAINIAN AMERICAN

Ukrainian Institute of Modern Art

2320 W. Chicago Ave.
Chicago, IL 60622
(773) 227-5522

Contact:
Orysia Cardoso
pres.
Email: info@uima-chicago.org

Purpose:
To serve the community as an educational art center.

Programs:
Permanent art collection, periodic art exhibits, concerts and literary evenings.

Website: www.uima-chicago.org

Ukrainian National Museum

2249 W. Superior St.
Chicago, IL 60612
(773) 421-8020

Contact:
Jaroslaw Hankewych
pres.
Email:
info@ukrainiannationalmuseum.org

Purpose:
To increase ethnic sensitivity in a changing world, promote Ukrainian history and culture, and serve as an educational resource.

Programs:
Library, archives available for research, educational programs and speakers.

Website: www.ukrainiannationalmuseum.org

VIETNAMESE AMERICAN

Vietnamese Association of Illinois

5110 N. Broadway
Chicago, IL 60640
(773) 728-3700

Contact:
Shara Chau
interim exec. dir.
Email: infovai@hnvi.org

Purpose:
To provide social services for the Vietnamese community and residents of the North Side of Chicago.

Programs:
Counseling, citizenship, community center, culture preservation, economic development, health education, literacy, referral, senior citizens, technical assistance, tutoring, women, youth, translating.

Website: www.hnvi.org

MULTI-ETHNIC

American Friends Service Committee

637 S. Dearborn – 3rd Floor
Chicago, IL 60605
(312) 427-2533

Contact:
Michael McConnell
exec. dir.
Email: MMcConnell@afsc.org

Purpose:
To develop leadership from within the peace and justice movement that will include members from the diverse communities of Chicago, and to build a sustainable peace-with-justice movement that reaches beyond Chicago.

Programs:
Community organizing of Taxi Workers; Truth in Recruitment to Chicago Public High Schools; education and organizing about Afghanistan and Iraqi wars and U.S. military budget; organizing Palestinian community and college students to push for divestment from corporations working in Israel.

Website: www.afsc/chicago.org

Chicago Area Ethnic Resources

2231 Janet Drive
Glenview, IL 60026
(847) 224-6360

Contact:
Jeryl Levin
pres.,
Cynthia Linton
edit.
Email: Jeryl@chicagoethnic.org
cynthia@chicagoethnic.org

Purpose:
To research and publish information on the Chicago area's diverse ethnic, racial and cultural communities in an effort to better promote outreach, education and collaboration on issues impacting the region.

Programs:
Publishes the Directory of Chicago Area Ethnic Organizations and the Ethnic Handbook for the Chicago Area

Website: www.chicagoethnic.org

Coalition of African, Arab, Asian, European and Latino Immigrants of Illinois (CAAAELII)

4300 N Hermitage
Chicago, IL 60613
(773) 248-1019

Contact:
Lhakpa Tsering
Email: info@caaaelii.org

Purpose:
Advocating for immigrant and refugee rights.

Programs:
CIVITAS, human rights training, community health promoters, Street Vendors Campaign, 501(c)(3) Working Group. PRAXIS Institute.

Website: www.caaaelii.org

MULTI-ETHNIC

Chicago Cultural Alliance

4626 N. Knox
Chicago, IL 60630
(773) 283-1958

Contact:
Rebeccah Sanders
exec. dir.
Email: info@chicagoculturalalliance.org

Purpose:
To effect social change and public understanding of cultural diversity.

Programs:
Consortium of ethnic museums and cultural centers; public education; marketing ethnic events: providing organizational help to member agencies; cross-cultural public programs; capacity building workshops; shared services for member organizations, education resources.

Website: www.chicagoculturalalliance.org

Coalition of Limited English Speaking Elderly

53 W. Jackson Blvd., Suite 1301
Chicago, IL 60604
(312) 461-0812
Email: info@clese.org

Purpose:
To improve the lives of limited-English-speaking elderly by providing advocacy, leadership and education. Coalition of 50 agencies serving immigrant, refugee and migrant older adults.

Programs:
Bright ideas/ESL, community care, depression project, elder abuse, health, Medicare fraud, refugee project.

Website: www.clese.org

European American Assn.

2827 W. Division St.
Chicago, IL 60622
(773) 342-5868

Contact:
John Herman
exec. dir.
Email: webmail@eaachicago.org

Purpose:
To help neighborhood by offering social services.

Programs:
Homemaker (creating jobs while helping seniors remain independent), food pantry, energy assistance, senior home repair, community gardens, community development.

Website: www.eaachicago.org

MULTI-ETHNIC

Heartland Alliance for Human Needs & Human Rights

208 S. LaSalle St., Suite 1818
Chicago, IL 60604
(312) 660-1300

Contact:
Rev. Sid Mohn
pres.
Email: moreinfo@heartlandalliance.org

Purpose:
To advance human rights and respond to the human needs of endangered populations – particularly the poor, the isolated and the displaced – through comprehensive and respectful service and promotion of permanent solutions leading to a more just global society.

Programs:
Asset building, cross-cultural interpreting service, Heartland International Health Center, Marjorie Kovlar Center, national transitional job network, policy, advocacy, refugee health programs, Social IMPACT Research Center, Vital Bridges Center on Chronic Care, National Immigrant Justice Center.

Website: www.heartlandalliance.org

Illinois Coalition for Immigrant and Refugee Rights

55 East Jackson, Suite 2075
Chicago, IL 60604
(312) 332-7360

Contact:
Joshua Hoyt
exec. dir.
Email: josh@icirr.org

Purpose:
To promote immigrant and refugee rights to participate fully and equally in a diverse society in an increasingly interdependent world.

Programs:
Outreach and information, referral, advocacy, training and conference coordination.

Website: www.icirr.org

Legal Services Center for Immigrants

(Legal Assistance Foundation)
120 S. LaSalle Street
Chicago, IL 60603
(312) 341-1070

Contact:
Lisa J. Palumbo
supervising atty.

Purpose:
To provide low-income immigrants with affordable legal representation in deportation proceedings and in abused-spouse or child petitions; to provide brief legal advice and referral on other immigration cases.

Programs:
Legal advice, representation and referral.

MULTI-ETHNIC

RefugeeOne
(formerly Int'l Refugee & Immigration Ministries)
4753 N. Broadway, Suite 401
Chicago, IL 60640
(773) 989-5647

Contact:
Melineh Kano
pgm. dir.
Email: info@refugeeone.org

Purpose:
To create opportunities for refugees fleeing war, terror and persecution to build new lives of safety, dignity and self-reliance.

Programs:
Reception and placement, case management, employment assistance, English language training, computer training, refugee child and family outreach, immigration and citizenship assistance, elderly assistance, mental health assessments, fundraising and external relations.

Website: www.refugeeone.org

United Network for Immigrant & Refugee Rights
1808 S. Blue Island
Chicago, IL 60608
(312) 563-0002

Contact:
Oscar Tellez
exec. dir.
Email: unirjaguar@aol.com

Purpose:
To advocate for civil and human rights for immigrants.

Programs:
Citizenship, civil rights, labor rights, immigration, education, visa processing, referral, translating.

Universidad Popular
2801 S. Hamlin Ave
Chicago, IL 60623
(773) 733-5055

Contact:
Olivia Flores-Godinez
Email: up@universidadpopular.us

Purpose:
Community empowerment.

Programs:
Adult education through English and computer classes, Uprising Youth program for ages 11-17, health literacy, financial literacy, familiy literacy.

Website: www.universidadpopular.us

MULTI-ETHNIC

World Relief Chicago
3507 W. Lawrence Ave.
Chicago, IL 60625
(773) 583-9191

Contact:
Nora Brathol
Email: chicago@wr.org

Purpose:
To provide services that address the needs of refugees, immigrants and other newcomers to our community.

Programs:
Refugee resettlement and adjustment, ESL education, accredited immigrant legal services.
Additional location: Wheaton

Website: www.worldrelief.org/chicago

GOVERNMENT AGENCIES

Cook County Commission on Human Rights
69 W. Washington St., Suite 3040
Chicago, IL 60602
(312) 603-1100

Contact:
MaryNic Foster
exec. dir.
Email:
human.rights@cookcountyil.com

Purpose:
To enforce ordinance prohibiting discrimination in employment, housing, credit and public accommodations in Cook County.

Programs:
Civil rights law enforcement, educational programs on preventing harassment and discrimination, civil rights compliance and improving intergroup relations.

Website: www.cookcountygov.com

Illinois Dept. of Human Rights
100 W. Randolph St., Suite 10-100
Chicago, IL 60601
(312) 814-6200

Contact:
Hector Villagrana
Email: idhr.webmail@illinois.gov,
hector.villagrana@illinois.gov

Purpose
To investigate charges alleging discrimination against people based on race, religion, color, sex and any other biases that prevent equal rights and opportunities.

Programs:
Investigation, seminars, speakers.

Website: www.state.il.us/dhr/

GOVERNMENT AGENCIES

Illinois Department of Human Services, Bureau of Refugee & Immigrant Services

401 S. Clinton
Chicago, IL 60607
(312) 793-7120

Contact:
Dr. Edwin B. Silverman
bureau chief

Purpose:
To expedite refugee resettlement and facilitate citizenship.

Programs:
Counseling, employment, adjustment, instruction, health and mental health for refugees.

Office of New Americans

Mayor's Office, City Hall
121 N. LaSalle St., Room 406
Chicago, IL 60602
(312) 744-5201

Contact:
Adolfo Hernandez
dir. (312) 545-5309
Email:
aldolfo.hernandez@cityofchicago.org

Purpose:
To make Chicago the most immigrant-friendly city in the world.

Programs:
To partner with community organizations, educational institutions and the private sector to expand opportunities of immigrant business owners, enhance coordination between City government and community organizations, improve language capabilities of City departments, Expand English language education in community settings, expand immigrant parent engagement in public school, support launch of Illinois DREAM Act with scholarships, promote U.S. citizenship.

ETHNIC MEDIA

AFRICAN AMERICAN MEDIA

African-American Reader

(773) 568-2274

Contact:
Sam Henderson
edit. and pub.
Email: thebonnetwork@gmail.com

Website: africanamericandaily.com

Published:
Monthly
Circulation:
10,000
Distributed:
Subscription and newsstands on Southeast Side and suburbs
Editorial focus:
Community news

Austin Voice

5236 W. North Ave.
Chicago, IL 60639
(773) 889-0880

Contact:
Brad Cummings
assoc. edit.
Email: tvoicenews@sbcglobal.net

Website: www.thevoicenewspaper.blogspot.com

Published:
Weekly
Circulation:
18,000
Distributed:
Austin & Galewood
Editorial focus:
Neighborhood news

Black Online News Network

P.O. Box 28-8482
Chicago, IL 60628
(773) 568-2274
Email: thebonnetwork@gmail.com

Website: www.thebonngroup.com

Editorial focus:
Newswire for African American community

AFRICAN AMERICAN MEDIA

The Chicago Citizen Newspaper Group

806 E. 78th St.
Chicago, IL 60619
(773) 783-1251

Contact:
Lisette Livingston
edit.-in-chief
Email: info@thechicagocitizen.com

Website: www.thechicagocitizen.com

Published:
Weekly
Circulation:
121,000
Distributed:
Suburban Chicago - South: Harvey, Markham, Robbins, Dixmoor, Calumet Park, Phoenix, Blue Island, South Holland and Alton
Editorial focus:
Community news
Publications:
Chatham-Southeast, South End, Chicago Weekend, Hyde Park and South Suburban Citizen

Chicago Crusader

6429 S. King Drive
Chicago, IL 60637
(773) 752-2500

Contact:
Dorothy Leavell
edit. and pub.
Email: achicagocrusader@aol.com

Website: www.chicagocrusader.com

Published:
Weekly
Circulation:
146,000
Distributed:
Chicago & Gary, Ind.
Editorial focus:
Black community

Chicago Defender

4445 S. King Dr.
Chicago, IL 60653
(312) 225-2400

Contact
Kathy Chaney
man. edit.
Email: editorial@chicagodefender.com

Website: www.chicagodefender.com

Published:
Weekly
Circulation:
30,000
Distributed:
Chicago
Editorial focus:
Community news

AFRICAN AMERICAN MEDIA

Chicago South Shore Scene

7433 S. Constance
or
P.O. Box 49008
Chicago, IL 60649
(773) 363-0441

Contact:
Valencia Rias
edit.
Email:
vawinsteadservices@yahoo.com

Published:
Weekly
Circulation:
80,000
Distributed:
Chicago's South East Side to Indiana state line
Editorial focus:
Chicago - South

Final Call Newspaper

734 W. 79th St.
Chicago, IL 60620
(773) 602-1230

Contact:
Richard Muhammad
edit.
Email: fcnprod@aol.com

Website: www.finalcall.com
Published:
Weekly
Circulation:
900,000
Distributed:
Nationwide
Editorial focus:
Black Muslim news and commentary

Garfield-Lawndale Voice

5236 W. North Ave.,
Chicago, IL 60639
(773) 889-0880

Contact:
Brad Cummings
assoc. edit.
Email: tvoicenews@sbcglobal.net

Website: www.thevoicenewspapers.blogspot.com
Published:
Weekly
Circulation:
18,000
Distributed:
East & West Garfield Park, North Lawndale, West Humboldt Park, West Haven, Near West Side
Editorial focus:
Neighborhood news

AFRICAN AMERICAN MEDIA

The South Street Journal Newspaper

449 E. 35th St.
Chicago, IL 60616
(312) 624-8351

Contact:
Ron Carter
edit. & pub.
Email: sostreetjournal@aol.com

Website: www.southstreetjournal.net

Published:
Bi-weekly
Circulation:
10,000
Distributed:
South Side, West Side, North Side
Editorial focus:
Community news

West Suburban Journal

490 Beloit Ave.
Forest Park, IL 60130
(708) 771-5975

Contact:
Nicole L. Trottie
pub.
Email: info@westsuburbanjournal.com

Website: www.westsuburbanjournal.com

Published:
Weekly
Circulation:
10, 000
Distributed:
West Suburban Chicago
Editorial focus:
Community news

Windy City Word

5090 W. Harrison St.
Chicago, IL 60644
(773) 378-0261

Contact:
Jocelyn Denson
edit.
Email: jdenson@ameritech.net

Website: www.windycityword.com

Published:
Weekly
Circulation:
20,000
Distributed:
West Side Chicago, from Fullerton to Roosevelt to Austin to Halstead
Editorial focus:
West Side/African-American community news and culture

AFRICAN AMERICAN MEDIA

WVON (1690 AM)
1000 East 87th St.
Chicago, IL 60619
Phone: (773) 247-6200

Contact:
Melody Spann-Cooper
gen. mgr.

Email:
precious@wvon.com, info@wvon.com

Website: www.wvon.com

Type of programming:
Talk, news, blues, international and current issues

ARAB AMERICAN MEDIA

The Arab Horizon
Amani Media Inc.
6000 W. 79th St., Suite 204,
Burbank, IL 60459
(708) 601-3731

Contact:
Amani Ghouleh
edit. & pub.
Email: aloffok@aol.com

Website: www.aloffok.com

Publishes:
Monthly
Circulation:
10,000
Distributed:
Chicago
Language:
English and Arabic

CHINESE AMERICAN MEDIA

Chicago Chinese News

424 Fort Hill Dr., Building #100,
Naperville IL 60540
(630) 717-4567

Contact:
Dany Lee
pub.
Email:
ccn100@chicagochinesenews.com

Website: www.chicagochinesenews.com

Published:
Bi-weekly
Circulation:
20,000
Distributed:
Chicago and suburbs
Editorial focus:
Community news
Language:
Chinese

China Journal

2146-A S. Archer Ave.
Chicago, IL 60616
(312) 326-3228

Contact:
May Zheng
pub.
Email: chinajournal@sbcglobal.net

Website: www.chinajournalus.com

Published:
Weekly
Circulation:
20,000
Distributed:
Chicago
Editorial focus:
Chicago and surrounding suburbs
Language:
Chinese

Chinese American News

733 W. 26th St.
Chicago, IL 60616-1854
(312) 225-5600

Contact:
James Chang
pub.
Email: editor@canews.com

Published:
Weekly
Circulation:
12,000
Distributed:
Metro Chicago area
Editorial focus:
Chinese American community
Language:
Chinese

CHINESE AMERICAN MEDIA

Sing Tao Daily

2134B S. China Place
Chicago, IL 60616
(773) 523 5888

Contact:
Rebecca Ip
edit.
Email: rebeccaip18@hotmail.com

Website: www.singtao.com

Published:
Daily
Circulation:
5,000
Distributed:
Retailers in Chinese communities
Editorial focus:
Local, national, international news
Language:
Chinese

The World Journal

1334 Enterprise Dr.
Romeoville, IL 60446
(630) 759-9880

Contact:
Katie Chang
mgr. & edit.
Email: katiechang@worldjournal.com

Website: http://204.2.119.85/

Published:
Daily
Circulation:
3,600
Distributed:
Midwest
Editorial focus:
Chinese community news
Language:
Chinese

DANISH AMERICAN MEDIA

Den Danske Pioneer
(The Danish Pioneer)
1582 Glen Lake Rd.
Hoffman Estates IL 60169
(847) 882-2552

Contact:
Elsa Steffensen
pub.
or
Chris Steffensen,
edit.
Email: dpioneer@aol.com

Website: http://www.dendanskepioneer.com/

Published:
26 times/year
Circulation:
3,500
Distributed:
By subscription only in USA, Denmark, Canada
Editorial focus:
Denmark news and politics, USA coverage
Language:
Danish and English

FILIPINO AMERICAN MEDIA

The Philippine Weekly
P.O. Box 68593
Schaumburg, IL 60168
(847) 352-3877

Contact:
Orlando P. Bernardino
pub. & edit.
Email: philweekly@ameritech.net

Website: http://www.thephilippineweekly.com/

Published:
Weekly
Circulation:
15,000
Distributed:
Chicago area
Editorial focus:
News of Philippines and Chicago's Filipino community
Language:
English, Tagalog

FILIPINO AMERICAN MEDIA

Philippine Time-USA Magazine
P.O. Box 6176
Buffalo Grove, IL 60089
(847) 466-5158

Contact:
Bart Tubalinal Jr.
edit.
Email: philtime@aol.com

Website: www.philtime-usa.com

Published:
Monthly
Circulation:
38,000
Distributed:
Chicago metro; by subscription elsewhere
Editorial focus:
Events in Philippines and local Filipino news
Language:
English and Pilipino

GERMAN AMERICAN MEDIA

German American Journal
c/o German American National Congress
4740 N. Western Avenue, Suite 206,
Chicago, IL 60625
(773) 275-1100

Contact:
Darlene Fuchs
edit.
Email: office@dank.org/journal/

Website: http://www.dank.org/journal/

Published:
Bi-monthly
Circulation:
4,000
Distributed:
Nationwide
Editorial focus:
Organization news, news affecting German Americans, current events, business, travel
Language:
German

GERMAN AMERICAN MEDIA

Eintracht

9456 N. Lawler Ave.
Skokie, IL 60077-1290
(847) 679-0599

Contact:
Walter & Klaus Juengling
Email: eintracht@aceweb.com

Published:
Weekly
Circulation:
5,000
Distributed:
By subscription in Chicago and suburbs, other states and overseas.
Editorial focus:
World political news, sports, happenings in German American circles.
Language:
German

GREEK AMERICAN MEDIA

Greek Press

4849 N. Milwaukee, Suite 103
Chicago, IL 60630
(773) 663-0209

Contact:
Ernest Panos
pub.
Bob Nicolaides
edit.
Email: thegreekpress@yahoo.com

Website: http://www.greekpressonline.com/

Published:
Monthly and online
Circulation:
13,000
Distributed:
By subscription only in Chicago and suburbs
Editorial focus:
News pertaining to Greek American community
Language:
99% English, 1% Greek

GREEK AMERICAN MEDIA

Greek Star

4727 N. Lincoln Ave., Suite 4
Chicago, IL 60625
(773) 989-7211

Contact:
Diane Adam
Email: greek1@mac.com

Website: http://thegreekstar.com/

Published:
Weekly by the United Hellenic American Congress
Circulation:
7,200
Distributed:
By subscription only in Chicago area and nationwide
Editorial focus:
Local Greek American community
Language:
English

HISPANIC/LATINO MEDIA

El Dia

6331 W. 26th St.
Berwyn, IL 60402
(708) 652-6397

Contact:
Ana Maria Montes de Oca
edit.
Email: anamaria@eldianews.com

Website: www.eldianews.com

Published:
Weekly
Circulation:
60,000
Distributed:
Chicago and suburbs
Editorial focus:
National and local Hispanic community
Language:
70% Spanish, 30% English

HISPANIC/LATINO MEDIA

El Imparcial

3116 S. Austin Blvd.,
Cicero, IL 60804
(708) 656-6666 (x1074 for ed.)

Contact:
America Vazquez
edit.
Email: avazquez@teleguia.us

Website: www.elimparcial.us

Publishes:
Weekly
Circulation:
10,000
Distributed:
Supermarkets banks, clinics, restaurants and street boxes in Chicago, Berwyn, Cicero, Melrose Park
Editorial focus:
Local news, sports, arts, national and international news
Language:
Spanish and English

Extra

3906 W. North Ave.
Chicago, IL 60647
(773) 252-3534

Contact:
Mila Tellez
pub.
Email: info@extranews.com, mila@extranews.net

Website: www.extranews.net

Publishes:
Weekly
Circulation:
67,500
Distributed:
Boxes in Chicago, suburbs
Editorial focus:
Community news
Language:
Spanish and English

Hoy

435 N. Michigan Ave., 12nd floor
Chicago, IL 60611
(312) 527-8400

Contact:
Fernando Diaz
edit.
Email: fdiaz@tribune.com

Website: http://www.vivelohoy.com/

Publishes:
Daily
Circulation:
Varies 62,000-300,000
Distributed:
Chicago, Illinois
Language:
Spanish
Weekend edition:
Fin de Semana

HISPANIC/LATINO MEDIA

Lawndale News

5533 W. 25th St.
Cicero, IL 60804
(708) 656-6400

Contact:
Gary Miller
edit. (x115)
Email: gm@lawndalenews.com

Website: http://www.lawndalenews.com/

Publishes:
Twice a week
Circulaxtion:
188,000
Distributed:
Chicago, Cicero, Berwyn, other suburbs
Editorial focus:
Community
Language:
English and Spanish

Nuevo Siglo

2644 W. 47th St.
Chicago, IL 60632
(773) 890-1656

Contact:
Ezequiel Banda Sifuentes
edit.
Email: ebanda@nuevosiglionews.com

Website: http://www.nuevosiglonews.com/

Publishes:
Weekly
Circulation:
30,000
Distributed:
Chicago, Cicero, Berwyn
Editorial focus:
Community issues, local and national news
Language:
Spanish

La Raza

225 W. Ohio St., Suite 300
Chicago, IL 60654
(773) 273-2900

Contact:
Jesus Del Toro
editor-in-chief
Email: agenda@laraza.com

Website: www.laraza.com

Publishes:
Weekly by Intermedia
Circulation:
152,000
Distributed:
Chicago and suburbs
Editorial focus:
Hispanic community
Language:
Spanish

HISPANIC/LATINO MEDIA

Reflejos Publications, LLC

155 E. Algonquin Rd.
Arlington Heights, IL 60005
(847) 806-1111

Contact:
Marco Ortiz
content edit.

Email:
copy@reflejos.com,
mortiz@reflejos.com

Website: http://www.reflejos.com/

Publishes:
Weekly

Circulation:
230,000

Distributed:
Chicago Northwest suburbs

Editorial focus:
Hispanic community news, national news relevant to Hispanics

Languages:
Spanish, English and bilingual

Teleguia de Chicago

3116 S. Austin
Cicero, IL 60804
(708) 656-6666

Contact:
Martha Saldana
edit.

Email: msaldana@teleguia.com,
info@teleguia.us

Website: http://teleguia.us/

Publishes:
Weekly

Circulation:
38,000

Distributed:
Chicago and some suburbs

Editorial focus:
Spanish entertainment

Language:
Spanish

Univision Chicago (WGBO)

541 N. Fairbanks Court
Chicago, IL 60611
(312) 494-2742

Contact:
Luisa Echevarria
pub. affairs dir.

Email: lechevarria@univision.com

Website: www.univision.com

Broadcast:
Chicago area

Editorial focus:
News, current events for Hispanic Americans

Language:
Spanish

HISPANIC/LATINO MEDIA

WLEY (107.9 FM) La Ley

150 N. Michigan Ave., Suite 1040
Chicago, IL 60601
(312) 920-9500

Contact:
Joe Mackey
gen. mgr.
Email: jmackay@sbschicago.com, info@laley1079.com

Website: http://www.laley1079.com/

Broadcast:
Chicago

Type of programming:
Regional Mexican music

Language:
Spanish

WNUA Mega 95.5-FM

233 N. Michigan Ave., Suite 2800
Chicago, IL 60601
(312) 540-2000

Contact:
Ricardo Otero
pgm. dir.
Email: gonzo@clearchannel.com

Website: www.wnua.com

Listeners:
825,000

Broadcast:
Chicago metro area

Editorial focus:
Latino music

Language:
Spanish

WOJO (105.1 FM)

625 N. Michigan Ave.
Chicago, IL 60611
(312) 981-1800

Contact:
Jerry Ryan
gen. mgr. and V.P.
Email: jerryryan@univision.com

Website: www.univision.com

Broadcast:
Chicago metro area

Editorial focus:
Spanish music

Language:
Spanish

WPPN (106.7 FM)

625 N. Michigan Ave., Suite 300
Chicago, IL 60611
(312) 981-1800

Contact:
Jerry Ryan
sr. V.P. and gen. mgr.
Email: jerryryan@univisionradio.com

Website: www.univisionradio.com

Editorial focus:
Adult contemporary music

Language:
Spanish

HISPANIC/LATINO MEDIA

WRTE-FM Radio Arte

1401 W. 18th St.
Chicago, IL 60608
(312) 455-9455

Contact:
Carlos Mendez
pgm. dir.
Email: carlos.mendez@radioarte.com

Website: www.wrte.org

Editorial focus:
Young Latino interest, Mexican fine arts
Language:
Spanish, English

WRTO 1200 AM

625 N. Michigan Ave., Suite 300
Chicago, IL 60611
(312) 981-1800

Contact:
Doug Levy
sta. mgr.
Email: dlevy@univision.com

Website: www.univisionradio.com

Type of programming:
Spanish talk/news
Language:
Spanish

WRZA (99.9 FM) and WSNS-TV (Ch. 44)

454 N. Columbus Drive
Chicago, IL 60611
(312) 836-3000

Contact:
John Alfonzo
pgm. dir.
Email: john.alfonzo@nbcuni.com

Website: www.telemundochicago.com

Type of programming:
News, talk, public service
Languages:
English and Spanish

INDIAN MEDIA

India Bulletin

P.O. Box 59584
Chicago, IL 60659
(847) 674-7941

Contact:
Ron Shah
edit.
Email: ron@indiabulletinusa.com

Website: www.indiabulletinusa.com

Publishes:
Bi-weekly
Circulation:
28,000
Distributed:
Illinois
Editorial focus:
News affecting South Asia
Language:
English

India Tribune

3302 W. Peterson Ave.
Chicago, IL 60659
(773) 588-5077

Contact:
Prashant Shah
founding pub. & dir.
Email: prashant@indiatribune.com

Website: www.indiatribune.com

Published:
Weekly on Fridays
Circulation:
48,000
Distributed:
USA
Editorial focus:
News of India and Indian community in the USA
Language:
English

IRISH MEDIA

Irish American News

7115 W. North Ave., Suite 327
Oak Park, IL 60302
(708) 445-0700

Contact:
Cliff Carlson
edit. & pub.
Email: editor@ianews.com

Website: www.irishamericannews.com

Published:
Monthly
Circulation:
15,000
Distributed
Chicago area 95%
Editorial focus:
Local news and current events for the Irish community, poetry, sports, entertainment, history, books
Language:
English

ITALIAN MEDIA

Fra Noi

3800 Division St.
Stone Park, IL 60165
(708) 338-0690

Contact:
Paul Basile
edit.
Email: franoinews@aol.com

Website: www.franoi.com

Published:
Monthly
Circulation:
10,000
Distributed:
Metropolitan Chicago
Editorial focus:
News and features about Italians and Italian Americans in Chicago, USA and Italy
Language:
English and Italian

JAPANESE MEDIA

Chicago Shimpo

4670 N. Manor Ave.
Chicago, IL 60625
(773) 478-6170

Contact:
Yoshiko Urayama
edit.
Email: shimpo@mc.net

Published:
Friday
Circulation:
5,000
Distributed:
Subscribers and stores in Chicago area
Editorial focus:
Local news and national news affecting the local community
Language:
Japanese and English

JEWISH MEDIA

Chicago Jewish News

5301 W. Dempster St.
Skokie, IL 60077
(847) 966-0606

Contact:
Pauline Yearwood
man. edit. (x13)
Email: paulinecjn@aol.com

Website: www.chicagojewishnews.com

Publishes:
Weekly
Circulation:
40,000
Distributed:
Chicago and suburbs
Editorial focus:
Jewish community in Chicago; national and international news
Language:
English

JEWISH MEDIA

JUF News

30 S. Wells St.
Chicago, IL 60606
(312) 357-4848

Contact:
Cindy Sher
edit.
Email: jufnews@juf.org

Website: www.juf.org

Published:
Monthly by Jewish United Fund

Circulation:
45,000

Distributed:
By mail to those who contribute $10 to Jewish United Fund

Editorial focus:
Chicago's Jewish community and Israel

Language:
English

KOREAN MEDIA

Korea Daily News

790 Busse Road
Elk Grove Village, IL 60007
(847) 228-7200

Contact:
ChunHo Park
sr. reporter
Email: Chicago@koreadaily.com

Website: www.koreadaily.com

Published:
Daily

Circulation:
50,000

Distributed:
Midwest

Editorial focus:
Korean and Korean-American News

Language:
Korean

KOREAN MEDIA

Korean News of Chicago
(Kyocharo USA LLC)

3520 Milwaukee Ave., 2nd floor
Northbrook, IL 60062
(847) 391-4112

Contact:
Kim Nam and David Oh
Email: koreannewsusa@yahoo.com

Website: www.joinchicago.com

Published:
Monday and Thursday
Circulation:
7,000
Distributed:
Midwest
Editorial focus:
Korean community
Language:
Korean

Chicago Radio Korea – WKTA 1330 AM
(DBA Korea Broadcasting & Publishing Inc.)

2454 E. Dempster St.,
Suite 207
Des Plaines, IL 60016

Contact:
Thomas Kim
gen. mgr.
Email: am1330@ymail.com

Website: www.chicagoradiokorea.com

Type of programming:
News, K-pop music, world music, interview show, information
Language:
Korean

KBC-TV WOCH (Ch. 28)

5235 N. Kedzie
Chicago, IL 60625
(773) 588-0070

Contact:
Donald Bae
V.P. oper. (847) 674-0864
Email: kbchami@aol.com or
KBCTV41@gmail.com

Website: www.woch.net

Type of programming:
Drama, news
Language:
Korean

120

LITHUANIAN MEDIA

Cikagos Aidas
Lithuanian Newspaper

704 S. Milwaukee Avenue
Wheeling, IL 60090
(847) 272-9222

Contact:
Kristina Bruzaite
edit., or
Jovita Kuznecova
Email: aida@aidas.us

Website: www.aidas.us

Publishes:
Weekly
Circulation:
5,500
Distributed:
Chicago and suburbs
Editorial focus:
Lithuanian community, events, news
Language:
Lithuanian

Draugas

4545 W. 63rd St.
Chicago, IL 60629
(773) 585-9500

Contact:
Dalia Cidzikaite
edit.

Website: www.draugas.org

Published:
Three times a week
Circulation:
4,000
Distributed:
Worldwide
Editorial focus:
Catholic-oriented, politics, religion, community in USA
Language:
Lithuanian

PAKISTANI MEDIA

Urdu Times

7450 Skokie Blvd. Suite 250
Skokie IL 60077
(773) 274-3100

Contact:
Tariq Khawaja
Email: urdutimes@hotmail.com

Website: www.urdutimesusa.com/chicago

Published:
Weekly by Times Publication
Circulation:
30,000
Distributed:
USA
Editorial focus:
Pakistanis and Indians
Language:
Urdu and English

POLISH MEDIA

Dziennik Zwiazkowy (Polish Daily News)

5711 N. Milwaukee Ave.
Chicago, IL 60646
(773) 763-3343

Contact:
Wojciech Bialasiewicz
edit.
Email: editorial@polishdailynews.com, dziennikzwiazkowy@gmail.com

Website: www.polishdailynews.com

Published:
Daily Mon.-Fri. by the Polish National Alliance
Circulation:
30,000
Distributed:
Chicago and suburbs and by subscription worldwide
Editorial focus:
General news, editorials, Polish American community, literature, history, arts, sports
Inserts:
Kalejdoskop, Angora, Dziennik Sportowy
Language:
Polish

POLISH MEDIA

Monitor

6615 W. Irving Park Road, Suite 202
Chicago, IL 60634
(773) 205-0303

Contact:
Jacek Zaworski
edit.-in-chief
Email: monitor@infolinia.com

Website: www.infolinia.com

Published:
Weekly by Monitor Publishing
Circulation:
20,000
Distributed:
Chicago and suburbs
Editorial focus:
Local news (Chicago area); cultural guide, immigration, real estate, health and education topics, classified ads
Language:
Polish

Narod Polski

984 Milwaukee Ave.
Chicago, IL 60642-4101
(773) 278-2600

Contact:
Kathryn Rosypal
exec. edit.
Email: kathryn.rosypal@prcua.org

Website: www.prcua.org

Distributed:
USA
Published:
Monthly by the Polish Roman Catholic Union of America (PRCUA)
Circulation:
23,000
Editorial focus:
News related to the Polish American community and PRCUA
Language:
Polish and English

Polonia Today Online

6348 N. Milwaukee Ave. #360
Chicago, IL 60646
(773) 763-1646

Contact:
T. Ron Jasinski-Herbert
edit.
Email: editor@poloniatoday.com

Website: http://www.poloniatoday.com

Published:
Monthly on the 15th
Circulation:
350,000 visitors to website per month
Distributed:
Worldwide (80% in USA)
Editorial focus:
Poland and Polish community worldwide
Language:
English

POLISH MEDIA

Polvision TV

3656 W. Belmont Ave.
Chicago, IL 60618
(773) 588-6300

Contact:
Agnieszka Pokropek
gen. mgr.
Email: advertising@polvision.com

Website: www.polvision.com

Type of programming:
Polish community in Chicago metro area
Language:
Polish

Zgoda

6100 N. Cicero Ave.
Chicago, IL 60646
(773) 286-0500

Contact:
Frank Spula
pres.
Email: frank.spula@pna-znp.org,
pna@pna-znp.org

Website: www.pna-znp.org/content/zgoda/zgoda2012.htm

Published:
Monthly by the Polish National Alliance
Circulation:
75,000
Distributed:
Nationwide
Editorial focus:
Newsletter style newspaper sent to the members of PNA with articles and information on the lodges and councils and PNA activities
Language:
English and Polish

RUSSIAN MEDIA

7 Days Russian Newspaper

704 S. Milwaukee Ave.,
Wheeling, IL 60090
(847) 272-2229

Contact:
Ilya Genn
edit.
Email: 7days@7days.us

Website: www.7days.us

Published:
Weekly
Circulation:
8,500
Distributed:
Illinois
Editorial focus:
Russian community, events, news
Language:
Russian

WEEF 1430
WZUR Media

The People's Wave of Chicago
310 Melvin Drive, Suite 17
Northbrook, IL 60062
(847) 480-0023

Contact:
Sergey Zatsepin
pgm. dir.
Email: through website

Website: www.radionvc.com

Type of programming:
news/talk/music
Language:
Russian

MULTI-ETHNIC MEDIA

WCEV (1450 AM)

5356 W. Belmont Ave.
Chicago, IL 60641-4103
(773) 282-6700

Contact:
Lucyna Migala
pgm. dir.
Email: wcev@wcev1450.com

Website: www.wcev.com

Ethnic groups:
Czech/Slovak/Moravians, African Americans, Irish, Latinos, Polish

Languages:
Czech, English, Irish, Polish, Spanish, Arabic

Type of programming:
Multi-ethnic

WCGO (1590 AM)

4357 N. Lincoln Ave.
Chicago, IL 60618
(847) 475-1590

Contact:
Gus Rios
gen. mgr.
Email: grios@1590wcgo.com

Website: www.1590wcgo.com

Broadcast:
Chicago metro area

Language:
Spanish, Korean, Assyrian, Russian, Haitian; no primary language

Editorial focus:
Ethnic news, music

WPNA (1450 AM)

408 S. Oak Park Ave.
Oak Park, IL 60302
(708) 848-8980

Contact:
Jerry Obrecki
pub. affrs.
Email: email@wpna1490am.com

Ethnic groups:
Polish, Ukrainian, Irish

Languages:
Polish, Ukrainian, English

Type of programming:
News, current public issues, weather, sports, talk, polka, blues, punk, pop and other popular music